The C2

Cycling Guide

2000/01

*Use this guide with the official route map
available from Sustrans 0117 929 0888*

Gina Farncombe

Curlew Press

7th Edition	*C2C National Cycle Route*
Edited by	Gina Farncombe
Published by	Curlew Press Crookwath Cottage Dockray, Penrith, Cumbria CA11 0LG 017684 82633
e-mail Web page	gfarncombe@aol.com cumbria.com.accom/cycling.htm
	© Curlew Press 2000 ISBN 1-901224-05-8
Distributed by	Cordee Books and Maps 3a de Montfort Street Leicester LE1 7HD Tel 0116 254 3579
Front cover Back cover	Philip Nixon Alistair Noblet of Holiday Lakeland Photograph by Ted Liddle

Contents

Accommodation place names (west-east)

INTRODUCTION

Welcome to the C2C B&B Guide. This guide is designed to be used with the C2C Sustrans Map obtainable from Sustrans, 35 King Street, Bristol BS1 4DZ, tel. 0117 929 0888.

Your hosts have all been chosen for their understanding of the cyclist's needs, a warm welcome, acceptance of muddy legs, a secure place for your bike and provision of a meal either with them or at a nearby pub. Have a great holiday!

Accommodation is listed from the West to East Coast, not only because the map works this way but also because cyclists benefit from the prevailing wind at their back. If at all possible, please book accommodation, meals and packed lunches in advance, and do not arrive unannounced expecting beds and meals to be available! If you have to cancel a booking, please give the proprietor as much notice as you can so that the accommodation can be re-let.

Your deposit may be forfeited: this is at the discretion of the proprietor.

Suggestions for additional addresses are most welcome, together with your comments.

Please note: the information given in the Guide was correct at the time of printing and was as supplied by the proprietors. No responsibility can be accepted by the Independent B&B Guide as to completeness or accuracy, nor for any loss arising as a result. It is advisable to check the relevant details when booking.

Where do I start the C2C ....?

The best way to cycle the C2C is from West to East coast. If you want to return to the West Coast via the Reivers Route the gradients will be to your advantage.

By Train
To get to Whitehaven or Workington by train you must change on to a local line at CARLISLE. The journey takes about 1 hour. It follows the coastline and is dramatic and spectacular. Remember, it is essential to book your bike on the train well in advance.

Train enquiries   0345 484 950
Cycle reservations   0345 125 625

Return by Train
From Sunderland, continue to cycle up the coast to the main-line station at Newcastle. Remember, the local train from Sunderland will only take a total of 2 bikes. You will need to make special arrangements for more bikes.

By Car
If you have to come by car most landladies will allow you to leave your vehicle with them. There is secure long-term car parking in Whitehaven; 'phone the TIC on 01946 852939, or use one of the taxi services on page 00 or cycle back on the Reivers Route!

Note   ***Back-up vehicles are strongly advised to use main roads in order to keep the C2C as traffic free as possible.***

C - 2 - C CYCLE ROUTE - WESTERN HALF

PENNINES

ALSTON
Leadgate
Garrigill
Gamblesby
Melmerby
Winskill
Langwathby
Renwick
Edenhall
Little Salkeld
PENRITH
Motherby
Penruddock
M6
Hutton
Newton Rigg
Ullswater
Skelton
Mungrisdale
Blencow
Greystoke
Berrier
Troutbeck
Dockray
St. John's in-the-Vale
KESWICK
Threlkeld
Thirlmere
Bassenthwaite Lake
Derwentwater
Thornthwaite
Braithwaite
COCKERMOUTH
Lorton
WORKINGTON
Loweswater
Crummock Water
Seaton
Ennerdale Bridge
WHITEHAVEN
Cleator Moor
CARLISLE
M6

N ←

km
20
10
0

6

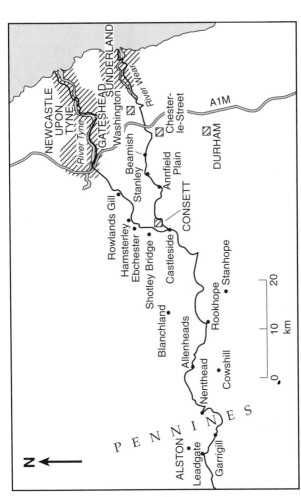

C - 2 - C CYCLE ROUTE - EASTERN HALF

TOPOGRAPHICAL CROSS-SECTIONS OF THE C-2-C CYCLE ROUTE

The C-2-C is 140 miles in length. It is strongly advised to ride the route from West to East, giving the benefit of the prevailing westerly winds at your back. As seen from the topographical sections, the uphill biking is short and sharp, and the downhill biking is long and gentle.

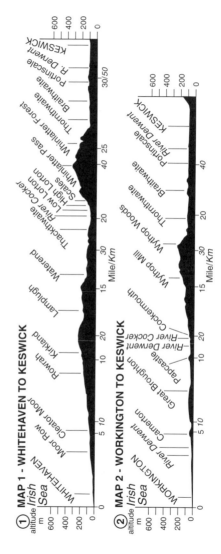

① MAP 1 - WHITEHAVEN TO KESWICK

② MAP 2 - WORKINGTON TO KESWICK

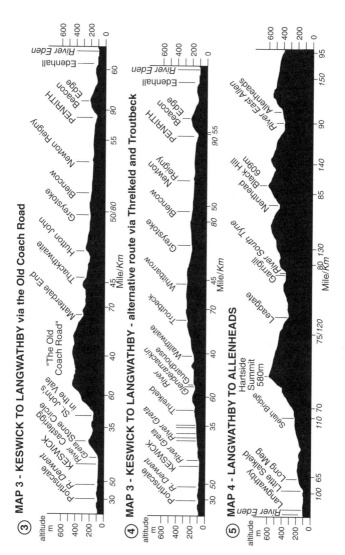

MAP 3 - KESWICK TO LANGWATHBY via the Old Coach Road

MAP 3 - KESWICK TO LANGWATHBY - alternative route via Threlkeld and Troutbeck

MAP 4 - LANGWATHBY TO ALLENHEADS

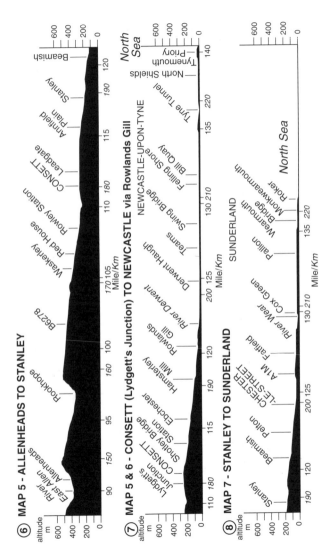

6 MAP 5 - ALLENHEADS TO STANLEY

7 MAP 5 & 6 - CONSETT (Lydgett's Junction) TO NEWCASTLE via Rowlands Gill

8 MAP 7 - STANLEY TO SUNDERLAND

WHITEHAVEN

Whitehaven bay

The town reached its peak of prosperity in the 1740s and 50s with outward trade of coal to Dublin and imports of tobacco from America and rum and sugar from the West Indies. There were early connections with the slave trade together with people settling in America. It was the third busiest port after London and Bristol. The Lowther family laid out the grid pattern

for the Georgian town in the late 1690s. Whitehaven's most notable scientist was William Brownrigg who studied the explosive mine-gas "fire damp". George Washington's grandmother, Mildred Warner Gale, lived in Whitehaven. Don't forget to dip your bike wheel in the Irish Sea! There is a convenient slipway on the harbour front.

The Beacon Visitor Centre

Whitehaven Tourist Information

PLACES OF INTEREST

Michael Moon's,   Bookshop & Gallery: largest bookshop
  Roper Street   in Cumbria, "vast and gloriously
                        eccentric!"

The Beacon   Local maritime and industrial history
                        within the Harbour Gallery

EATING OUT

Casa Romana   132 Queen St., Good food & fun
                        01946 591901

St Nicholas Centre St Nicholas Gardens, Lowther St
                        01946 64404

The New Expresso 22 Market Place: will do sandwiches
                        to order. Please phone 01946 591548

CYCLE SHOPS

Kershaw's Cycles 125 Queen Street 01946 590700
Mark Taylor Cycles 5/6 New Street 01946 692252

C2C Route Features: *as you leave Whitehaven you will join the Whitehaven-Rowrah cycle path which links the sea to the fells. The railway line was built in the 1850s to carry limestone, coal and iron; it is now a sculpture trail interpreting the geology and industrial history of the region. Further down the C2C the route takes you past the* **Whinlatter Visitor Centre**, *between Lorton and Braithwaite. Here you are in the midst of England's only mountain forest. It contains a wealth of forest habitat information and is well worth a visit if time and energy allow. They have a good tea room too.*

Whitehaven

Mrs Armstrong

Glen Ard Guest House, Inkerman Terrace, Whitehaven, CA28 7TY

Telephone	**01946 692249**
Rooms	2 single + 2 double + 2 twin + family
B&B	£15.00
Packed lunch	£3.50
Distance from C2C	¼ mile Pub nearby

"Family-run guest-house with a private car park only ¼ mile from the C2C route. Early breakfast available if requested."

T. Todd

The Mansion, Old Woodhouse, Whitehaven, Cumbria CA28 9LN

Telephone	**01946 61860** Fax 01946 691270
Rooms	10 double rooms *(8 en-suite)*
B&B	From £12.00 - £15.00
Evening meal	£4.00-£7.00 Packed Lunch £3.00
Distance from C2C	600m Pub nearby

"Recently renovated Georgian residence. Sauna, Jacuzzi and sunbed available. Friendly and informal. Courtesy pick-up if needed, off-street parking."

Joyce Bailey

The Cross Georgian Guest House, Sneckyeat Road, Hensingham, Whitehaven, CA28 8JQ

Telephone	**01946 63716**
Rooms	2 double (1 family) + 2 single
B&B	£15.00-£20.00 Packed lunch £2-3.00
Distance from C2C	On route Pub nearby

"A family-run guest-house on the outskirts of Whitehaven. En-suite rooms with Sky TV. Long-term spacious parking is available by arrangement. Lockable storage for bikes."

Whitehaven

Mrs C. M. Oliver Glenlea House, Glenlea Hill, Lowca,
Whitehaven, Cumbria CA28 6PS

Telephone **01946 693873** Fax 01946 694350
Rooms 3 single + 4 double + 4 twin + 1 family
B&B £15.00 - £19.00
Evening meal £8.50-£10.50 Packed lunch £3.50
Distance from C2C On route Pub 1 mile

*Family-run licensed guest-house. Private car park. Early
breakfast available for those wishing to make the most of the
day. We are happy to pick up cyclists from the station."*
(See advertisement on page 77)

Waverley Hotel Tangier Street, Whitehaven, Cumbria
CA28 7UX

Telephone **01946 694337** Fax 01946 691577
Rooms 10 single + 10 double
B&B From £20.00 - £37.00
Evening meal Available Packed lunch available
Distance from C2C ¼ mile Licensed restaurant

*"300-year-old hotel in centre
of historic Whitehaven. All
rooms have colour TV and
tea/coffee-making facili-
ties. Very near to bus
and train station."*

WORKINGTON

Helena
Thompson
Museum

Some parts of the town date back to Roman times. Local iron and steel-making helped Workington to expand into a major industrial 18th-century town and port. Famous names linked to the town are Henry Bessemer who introduced his revolutionary steel-making process and Mary Queen of Scots who sheltered in Workington Hall in 1568 on her flight from Scotland. The Hall is now ruined, but is open in summer and is a short distance from the Helena Thompson Museum.

PLACES OF INTEREST

Helena Thompson Museum Park End Road: a local history gallery together with the famous Clifton dish.

Workington Hall Apparently haunted by Henry Curwen!

EATING OUT

Impressions 173 Vulcans Lane: Good traditional English food 01900 605446

Super Fish 20 Pow St 01900 604916

CYCLE SHOPS

Traffic Lights Bikes 35 Washington St 01900 603283

New Bike Shop 18-20 Market Place 01900 603337

15

Workington

Mrs Caroline Nelson	Morven House Hotel, Siddick Road, Workington, Cumbria CA14 1LE
Telephone/Fax	**01900 602118**
Rooms	6 twin/double + 2 single
B&B	£19.50-£24.00
Evening meal	£10.00 Packed lunch £4.00
Distance from C2C	On route Pub nearby

ETB 3 diamonds *"A relaxed, informal atmosphere, an ideal stopover for C2C participants near start. Car park and secure cycle storage."* **(See advertisement on page 76.)**

Mrs Hazel Hardy	Silverdale, 17 Banklands, Workington, Cumbria CA14 3EL
Telephone	**01900 61887**
Rooms	2 twins + 2 single
B&B	£13.50-£15.00
Packed lunch	Available on request
Distance from C2C	On route Pub nearby

(No smoking in bedrooms please.) *"Large Victorian house, quiet location, wash-basins in all bedrooms, bathroom has shower, comfy TV lounge, centrally placed, good parking."*

Ennerdale Bridge

Mr Norman Stanfield	The Shepherds Arms Hotel, Ennerdale Bridge, Cleator, Cumbria CA23 3AR
Telephone/Fax	**01946 861249**
Rooms	1 family + 3 double + 3 twin + 1 single
B&B	£27.00-£29.50
Evening meal	£3.00-£14.50
Distance from C2C	1¼ miles Hotel has Public Bar

2 Star Hotel. *"A small friendly hotel in a beautiful situation, real ale, secure cycle storage, drying facilities, open all year, all rooms en-suite or with private facilities."*

Lorton

Roger & Helen Humphries The Old Vicarage, Church Lane
Lorton, Culmbria, CA13 9UN

Telephone	**01900 85656 Fax 01900 85656**
Email	oldvicarage@compuserve.com
Rooms	4 doubles + 4 twins + family suite
B&B	£21.00 - £30.00
Evening meal	£15.00 Packed lunch £4.00
Distance from C2C	On route Pub ¼ mile

ETB 4 Diamonds/AA. *"Beautiful country guest house. Lovely en-suite rooms including four poster and family suite. Log fires. Excellent dinners & wine list. Local pub 5 minutes walk."*

Mrs Armstrong Terrace Farm, Lorton, Cockermouth,
Cumbria CA13 9TX

Telephone	**01900 85278**
Rooms	1 twin/single + 2 family
B&B	£19.00-£20.00
Distance from C2C	c. ½ mile Pub nearby

2 Diamonds Commended. *"Homely welcome at our family-run hill-farm set in secluded village location with superb Lakeland fell views. Good pub food within walking distance."*

Mrs C. Edmunds Meadow Bank, High Lorton,
Cockermouth, Cumbria CA13 9UG

Telephone/Fax	**01900 85315**
Rooms	1 double + 1 twin en-suite
B&B	£18.00-£19.00
Packed lunch	£3.00
Distance from C2C	300 yds Pub 1 mile

(No smoking please.) *"Comfortable detached house in picturesque village of Lorton, 4 miles from Cockermouth,10 from Keswick. Excellent , of a very high standard, most welcoming."*

COCKERMOUTH

Cockermouth Castle

One of only two "Gem Towns" in the Lake District, Cockermouth is full of fine Georgian architecture and is set on the confluence of two famous salmon rivers: the Derwent and the Cocker. The historic town of Cockermouth has long held an attraction for writers, poets and artists. It is the birthplace of William and Dorothy Wordsworth and has a bustling community air about it. The smell of brewing hops often pervades the air and makes a visit to the pub tempting! The town has had its fair share of troubled times from the Border Raiders and it played host to the fugitive Mary Queen of Scots.

Wordsworth House

Cockermouth

PLACES OF INTEREST

Castlegate House   Frequent exhibitions of interesting
contemporary artists 01900 822149

Printing House   'Hands on' experience!
Museum

EATING OUT

The Quince &   13 Castle St: award-winning
Medlar   vegetarian food 01900 823579

Cheers   Main St: Wholesome home-made
pasta and pizzas 01900 822109

CYCLE SHOPS

The Wordsworth   Main St 01900 822757
Hotel Bike Hire

Derwent Cycles   4 Market Place 01900 822113

C2C Route Features: take care of the very steep descent
through Wythop Woods down to Bassenthwaite lakeside.
Thornthwaite Gallery is well worth a visit.

Cockermouth

John and Susan Graham	Rose Cottage, Lorton Road, Cockermouth, Cumbria CA13 9DX
Telephone/Fax	**01900 822189**
Rooms	3 double + 3 twin + 2 family + 1 single *(all en-suite)*
B&B	£23.00-£30.00
3-course Dinner	£12.50-£15.00 Packed lunch £4.50
Distance from C2C	¼ mile Pubs nearby

(No smoking in bedrooms please.) **3 Diamonds Commended.**
"Converted 18th-c Inn, family-run, garden, private car park, secure bicycle storage, warm and friendly atmosphere."

Newlands Valley

Tish & Tex Gowing	The Swinside Inn, Newlands Valley, Keswick, Cumbria CA12 5UE
Telephone/Fax	**017687 78253**
Rooms	1 single, 2 doubles, 2 twins + 1 family
B&B	£20.00-£25.00
Evening meal	£5.00-£12.00 Packed lunch £3.50
Distance from C2C	0.5 miles

3 Diamonds. *"Superb location. Clean spacious bedrooms. Most en-suite. Excellent bar meals. Real logfires in winter. Drying room & secure bike shed with racks."*

Christine Simpson	Uzzicar Farm, Newlands, Keswick, Cumbria CA12 5TS **017687 78367**
Rooms	2 double + 1 twin
B&B	£15.00-£18.00 Packed lunch - Yes
Distance from C2C	1 mile Pub ½ mile

(No smoking please.) *"A warm welcome awaits you in the peaceful and beautiful Newlands Valley. All bedrooms have wash-basins, central heating, tea/coffee-making facilities."*

KESWICK

Derwentwater

Sandwiched between Derwentwater, Blencathra and Skiddaw, Keswick has a fantastic setting. It became prosperous in the 16th century due to the mining of copper, lead, silver and iron. Mining engineers were imported from Germany: they were treated with suspicion by the locals and forced to make their homes on Derwent Island, but they overcame the hostility as German surnames can still be found amongst the local population. Graphite discovered in Borrowdale in the 1500s gave birth to the famous Cumberland Pencil Company.

The Moot Hall (now the TIC)

Keswick Tourist Information

PLACES OF INTEREST

The Cumberland Pencil Museum	West of town centre 017687 73626
Cars of the Stars	Town centre: vintage cars of famous stars 017687 73757

EATING OUT

Lakeland Pedlar	By central car park: combined tea/bike shop 017687 74492
Maysons	Lake Rd: importers of Eastern goods and excellent food 017687 74104

CYCLE SHOPS

The Stores, Braithwaite	Mr Hindmarch does cycle repairs in the village of Braithwaite 017687 78273
Keswick Mountain Bikes	Behind Pencil Museum: they do hot-air ballooning too! 017687 75202

*C2C Route Features: the route follows the old railway line which crosses and re-crosses the beautiful river Greta. The alternative Old Coach Road route passes **Castlerigg**, a wonderful stone circle.*

Castlerigg Stone Circle

Keswick

Mrs Sharon Helling Beckside Guest House, 5 Wordsworth Street, Keswick, Cumbria CA12 4HU

Telephone	**017687 73093**
Rooms	double + 1 twin *+ 1 family (all en-suite)*
B&B	£19.50 Packed lunch £4.00
Evening meal	£11.00
Distance from C2C	500 yds Town 3 mins

(No smoking please.) **2 Crowns Commended. RAC and AA Highly Commended.** *"Close to town centre, small and homely, all tastefully decorated bedrooms have colour TV and tea/coffee facilities. Good hearty breakfasts for hungry cyclists.1 minute from route."*

The Proprietor Kings Arms Hotel, Main Street, Keswick, Cumbria CA12 5BL

Telephone	**017687 72083 Fax 017687 75550**
Rooms	7 double + 4 twin + 2 family
B&B	£29.00-£35.00
Evening meal	From £9.00 Packed lunch £4.50
Distance from C2C	On route Pub nearby

3 Crowns Commended ETB. 2 Stars AA. *"Very charming 17th-c two stars Coaching Inn, Keswick town centre. Traditional homecooking and also pizzeria restaurant available. Popular hotel bar with many draught beers and good pub food. Secure store for bicycles."*

Mrs K Wells Ivy Lodge, 32 Penrith Road, Keswick Cumbria CA12 4HA

Telephone	**017687 75747**
Rooms	2 double + 2 twin
B&B	£17.50-£22.50 Evening Meal
Distance from C2C	500 yds Town 3 mins

"Convenient for parks, theatre & lake. Superb en-suite bedrooms. Drying room & lock up for cycles.."

Keswick

The Proprietor   The Skiddaw Hotel, Main Street
Keswick, Cumbria CA12 5BN

Telephone	**017687 72071 Fax 017687 74850**
Rooms	16 double + 11 twin + 6 family +7 single
B&B	£35.00-£41.00
Evening meal	From £12.95 Packed lunch £4.50
Distance from C2C	On route

3 AA Star + 4 Crowns Highly commended. *"Keswick town centre. Very comfortable hotel with free in-house saunas. Superb restaurant and popular bar. Food and drinks served all day. Secure lock-up for bikes. No smoking bedrooms available."*

Graeme and Gill Winter   Rivendell, 23 Helvellyn Street, Keswick, Cumbria CA12 4EN

Telephone	**017687 73822 Fax 017687 72830**
Rooms	4 double + 2 twin + 1 family + 1single
B&B	£18.00-£20.00
Evening meal	£12.50 Packed lunch £4.00
Distance from C2C	On route Pub nearby

(No smoking please.) "Warm, comfortable accommodation. Hearty brekkies for all you bike trekkies. Secure storage and drying facilities. Launderette and phone just over the road."

Keswick

Sonja Meere Cranford House, 18 Eskin Street,
Keswick, Cumbria CA12 4DG

Telephone	**017687 71017** Fax: 017687 72335
e-mail	sonja@cranfordhouse.freeserve.co.uk
Rooms	2 single + 2 double + 2 twin
B&B	£16.00-£20 Packed lunch £3.00
Distance from C2C	On route Pub nearby

(No smoking please.) *"Friendly B&B accommodation in residential area, 5 minutes walk from town centre. Lounge with open fire. Drying facilities available."*

Bill and Derwentdale Guest House, 8 Blencathra
  Elizabeth Riding Street, Keswick, Cumbria CA12 4HP

Telephone	**017687 74187**.
Rooms	3 double + 2 single + 1 twin
B&B	£17.00-£20.50 *(some en-suite)*
Evening meal	£11.00 Packed lunch £4.50
Distance from C2C	On route Pub nearby

(No smoking please.) **3 Diamonds** *"Friendly, comfortable, centrally-heated guest-house. Colour TV, tea/coffeemaking facilities, hair dryers, vegetarian cooking, close to town centre."*

S. R. North Century House, 17 Church Street,
Keswick, Cumbria CA12 4DT

Telephone	**017687 72843**
Rooms	3 double + 1 twin + 1 family
B&B	£16.50-£19.50
Packed lunch	£3.00
Distance from C2C	On route Pub nearby

(No smoking please.) *"Lovely Victorian house offering private or en-suite facilities, with a warm and friendly welcome."*

Keswick

Louise Ellerton	Grassmoor Guest House, 10 Blencathra Street, Keswick, Cumbria CA12 4HP
Telephone	**017687 74008**
Rooms	1 single + 3 double + 1 family + 1 twin
B&B	£16.50-£19.50 Packed lunch £3.50
Distance from C2C	On route Pub nearby

Hotel & Caterers Association Inspection *"Comfortable, relaxed guest house, centrally located for town, lake, fells. Rooms with TV, tea/coffee. Generous breakfasts. Children welcome. Secure cycle storage." (No smoking please)*

G. Burn	Harvington House, 19 Church Street, Keswick, Cumbria CA12 4DX
Telephone	**017687 75582**
Rooms	2 single + 2 double + 1 twin
B&B	From £16.00
Distance from C2C	On route Pub 5 mins

Hotel & Caterers Association Inspection *"Do you need a C2C stopover, or a base for some excellent mountain biking? Friendly relaxed B&B, secure bike storage and hearty breakfasts. Then give us a call!" (No smoking please)*

Mrs B.J. Harbage	Glaramara Guest House, 9 Acorn St, Keswick, Cumbria CA12 4EA
Telephone/Fax	**017687 73216/75255**
Mobile	**0411 763 019**
Rooms	1 single + 2 doubles + 1 twin + 1 family
B&B	From £17.00-£22 Packed Lunch £3.00

"Cosy, warm guest house with en-suite & drying facilities. Bike hire & storage + minor spares/repairs. Owners are mountain bikers and have local knowlege of good cyling."

Threlkeld

Chris and Caroline Briggs Scales Farm Country Guest House, Scales, Threlkeld, Keswick, CA12 4SY

Telephone/Fax **017687 79660**
e-mail scales@scalesfarm.demon.co.uk
Rooms 3 double + 1 family + 2 twin
B&B From £24.00 Packed lunch £4.50
Distance from C2C On route Pub adjacent

ETB 2 Crown Highly Commended. *"A welcoming traditional fells farmhouse oozing charm and character. Superb views over the rolling Cumbrian fells. 100% deposit essential!"*

Scales

The white Horse Excellent pub for food & drink, no B&B

Mungrisdale

Melissa Townson The Mill Inn, Mungrisdale, nr Penrith, Cumbria CA11 0XR

Telephone/Fax **017687 79632**
e-Mail the_mill_inn@compuserve.com
Rooms 1 single + 3 double + 5 twin + 1 family
B&B £24.50-£29.50
Meals £4.00-£20.00, served all day
Packed lunch £3.95 Public Bar
Distance from C2C On new amended route

(Smoking in bar only please.) **3 Diamonds AA QQQ.** *"Traditional 16th-c Inn. Beautiful location. Log fire, warm welcome, Excellent accommodation, home-made food, and real ales. Lock-ups available. You will want to come back!"*

Swaledales

Troutbeck

Mrs Steele	Gill Head Farm, Troutbeck, nr Penrith, Cumbria, CA11 0ST
Telephone	**017687 79652 Fax 017687 79130**
Rooms	3 double + 2 twin *(all en-suite)*
B&B	From £19.50-£26.00
Evening meal	*(prior notice please)*
Packed lunch	£3.50 *(prior notice please)*
Distance from C2C	On route Pub nearby

"Our comfortable 17th-c farmhouse offers all guests a warm welcome with log fires, traditional farmhouse fayre and quality en-suite rooms with all facilities. Campsite with all facilites next door." **3 Diamonds. (See Advertisement on Page 77)**

Mrs Maureen Dix	Greenah Crag Farm, Troutbeck, nr Penrith, Cumbria CA11 0SQ
Telephone	**017684 83233**
Rooms	2 double + 1 twin *(en suite available)*
B&B	£16.50-£22.00
Packed lunch	£3.00 *(prior notice please)*
Distance from C2C	½ mile Pub 3/4 mile

(No smoking please.) *"A warm welcome in our 17th-c farmhouse, central heating, tea/coffee-making, TV lounge, bike lock-up."*

Greystoke

Mrs Jean Ashburner

Lattendales Farm, Berrier Road, Greystoke, nr Penrith CA11 0UE

Telephone **017684 83474**
Rooms 1 double + 2 twin
B&B £16.50-£17.50
Distance from C2C On route Pub nearby

(No smoking please.) "17th-c farmhouse of character with comfortable accommodation well recommended by cyclists. Interesting stone-built village with Greystoke Castle nearby."

Mrs Ann Cooper

Meldene, Icold Road, Greystoke, nr Penrith, Cumbria CA11 0UG

Telephone/Fax **017684 83856**
Rooms 1 double + 1 twin + 1 family
B&B £16.00-£18.00 Packed lunch £3.50
Distance from C2C On route Pub nearby

(No smoking please.) "Detached family home near village centre. Tea/coffee-making facilities in all rooms. Clothes dried. Secure garage for cycles."

Greystoke

Mark Thompson

The Boot and Shoe Inn, Greystoke, nr Penrith, Cumbria CA11 0TP

Telephone	**017684 83343**
e-mail	oldboot@compuserve.com
Rooms	1 double + 2 twin + 1 family
B&B	£20.0-£25.00
Evening meal	Available 1900-2100hrs £5.50-£7.00
Packed lunch	£3.00 *(prior notice please)*
Distance from C2C	On route Pub

*"An 18th-c coaching inn on main C2C route, situated in picturesque village of Greystoke."***(See advertisement on page 79)**

Mrs C Mole

Brathen, The Thorpe, Greystoke, nr Penrith, Cumbria CA11 0TJ

Telephone/Fax	**017684 83595**
Rooms	3 double + 1 twin
B&B	£16.50
Packed lunch	£3.50
Distance from C2C	On route Pub 500 yds

3 Crowns Commended.
"Converted barn on the outskirts of this quiet village. Comfortable accommodation and a hearty breakfast."

30

Motherby

Mrs Jackie Freeborn

	Motherby House, Motherby, nr Penrith, Cumbria CA11 0RS.
Telephone	**017684 83368**
e-mail	jacquie@enterprise.net
Rooms	2 family/twin B&B £17.00
Evening meal	£11.00 *(prior notice please)*
Packed lunch	£4.50 *(prior notice please)*
Distance from C2C	1 mile Pub less than 1 mile

"An 18th-c house. Warm and friendly, beamed lounge, log fires, drying facilities, safe storage for bikes, and good food. Muddy bikers welcome!" **(See advertisement on page 79.)**

Skelton

Douglas Clarke

	Balandra, Skelton, Penrtih, Cumbria, CA11 9TE
Telephone/Fax	**017684 84342**
e-mail	**dougclarke_1999@yahoo.com**
Rooms	1 family + 1 double + 1 twin
B&B	£17.50-£20.00
Evening Meal	£5.50-£10.00 Packed lunch £3.00
Distance from C2C	2 miles Pub nearby

"Situated in a friendly village. Comfortable accommodation with home cooking. Cycle repairs & secure storage for bikes. Please 'phone for quickest route to B&B."

Newton Rigg

William O'Donovan Newton Rigg Campus, University of Central Lancs. Penrith, Cumbria CA11 0AH

Telephone	**01768 863791**
e-mail	**info@newtonrigg.ac.uk**
Rooms	230 singles! + 2 doubles + 17 twin
B&B	From £14.00-£21.00
Evening meals	From £6.00 Packed lunch £3.50
Distance from C2C	On route Pub On site

Welcome Host. *"Standard en-suite rooms. Meals available to non-residents. Secure cycle sheds. Bar. Shops. Laundrette."*

What is a Millennium Milepost?

There are Millennium Mileposts along most of the National Cycle Network which was created by the charity Sustrans. The posts mark the openings of each new section of the 8,000 mile National Cycle Network, and by Midsummer's Day in the year 2000 there will be nearly 1,000 of them in place. There are metal

*discs with pictures em-
posts. They relate to the
also contain letters of a
collect copies of the discs
writing paper over the
over with a pencil or
will be able to apply
Sustrans souvenirs
ures. If you are re-
you can go further
the secrets of the*

*bossed on the mile
theme of Time, and they
secret code. If you
(by placing a sheet of
disc and rubbing all
wax crayon) you
for special
called Time Treas-
ally dedicated,
and try to solve
Time Trail Code!*

If you want to know more information about the Time Trail please write to Sustrans PO Box 21 Bristol BS99 2HA or 'phone 0117 929 0888

PENRITH

Known locally as the Red Town because of its sandstone buildings Penrith is a picturesque market town with traditional shops and friendly atmosphere. The town was the capital of Cumbria in the 9th and 10th centuries. It is overlooked by the famous Beacon which acted as a link for a communications chain that ran the length of the country, a useful early warning system when the Scots were on the rampage. Two old-world shops have survived in a time-warp: Grahams, Penrith's answer to Fortnum and Masons, and Arnisons, the drapers, established in 1740 and once the home of Wordworth's grandparents.

Until the end of the 14th-c the town had no water supply. In 1385 Bishop Strickland diverted Thacka Beck from the river Peterill and an environmentally aware agreement allowed the townspeople to draw daily only as much water from the Peterill as would flow through the eye of a millstone.

Penrith Castle dates from 1897 when an existing pele tower was crenellated. The area would certainly have witnessed some violent times from across the Borders in the past.

Penrith Tourist Information

PLACES OF INTEREST

Robinson's School Middlegate: TIC and Museum. Local history on show and regular exhibitions

St Andrew's Church The Giant's Grave in the Churchyard: legendary slayer of monsters from Inglewood Forest!

EATING OUT

The Narrowgate Coffee Shop The Narrows: best coffee in town 01768 862599

The Bewick Princes Street 01768 864764

A Taste of Bengal Stricklandgate 01768 891700

CYCLE SHOPS

Arragons' Brunswick Road 01768 890344

Halford's Near Station

*C2C Route Features: the Watermill at Little Salkeld, organic millers with art gallery and café. **Long Meg and her Daughters**, a pre-historic stone circle (don't dance on the Sabbath, you may be turned into one of these stones!). If you go through Melmerby don't miss the famous **Village Bakery**, the **Shepherds Inn** or the **Isis Gallery**.*

Long Meg and her Daughters

Penrith

Mrs Blundell Albany House, 5 Portland Place, Penrith, Cumbria CA11 7QN

Telephone/Fax	**01768 863072**
Rooms	1 family (sleeps 5) + 1 double + 3 triple
B&B	From £17.50 Packed lunch £3.75
Distance from C2C	On route Pub nearby

3 Diamonds ETB. AA QQQ. *"Mid-Victorian town house, spacious comfortable rooms, tea/coffee, colour/satellite TV, free clothes drying, secure indoor storage for cycles."*

Eileen Reid and Peter Sowerby Brandelhow Guest House, 1 Portland Place, Penrith, Cumbria CA11 7QW

Telephone	**01768 864470**
Rooms	4 double/twin + 1 family
B&B	£17.00-£20.00
Packed lunch	£3.50 *(prior notice please)*
Distance from C2C	On route Pub nearby

3 Diamonds ETB. *"Victorian town house on C2C route. Comfortable beds and a good English breakfast for the weary cyclist! Tea/coffee, colour TV, washing and drying facilities."*

Ann Clark The Friarage, Friargate, Penrith, Cumbria CA11 7XR

Telephone	**01768 863635**
Rooms	1 double + 1 twin + 1 single + 2 family
B&B	£16.00-£20.00
Packed lunch	Available on request
Distance from C2C	On route Pub nearby

4 Diamonds ETB *"Historic house. Clean, comfortable, spacious,tea/coffee-making facilities, colour TV, good breakfast, warm welcome. Open March to October."*

Penrith

Kim Mawer   Corney House, 1, Corney Place,
                       Penrith, Cumbria CA11 7PY
Telephone   **01768 867627**
e-mail   kimrose@microsoft.com
Bunkhouse Style   6 beds (mixed sex)
B&B   £10.00   On C2C route

*"Unique bunkhouse style accommodation in listed building
with good facilities."*

The Proprietor   The George Hotel, Devonshire St,
                       Penrith, Cumbria CA11 7SU
Telephone   **01768 862696**   Fax   01768 868223
Rooms   12 double+11 single+ 8 Twin+3 family
B&B   From £32.00-£35.00
Evening meal   From £9.95-£12.95
Packed lunch   £4.50   Distance from C2C   On route

3 AA Stars. *"17th-c 3-star Coaching Inn Penrith town centre.
A la carte and 3 course carvery dinners. Cosy Oak Bar
serving interesting bar meals & popular draught beers.
Selection of more than 30 malt whiskies. No smoking bedrooms available & no smoking in restaurant ."*

Mr and   Woodland House Hotel,
** Mrs Davies**   Wordsworth Street, Penrith, CA11 7QY
Telephone   **01768 864177**   Fax 01768 890152
e-mail   davies@woodlandhouse.co.uk.
Rooms   2 double + 3 single + 2 twins+1 family
                       (all en-suite)
B&B   £24.00-£29.50
Packed lunch   £3.50 *(prior notice please)*
Distance from C2C   On route   Pub nearby

(No smoking please.) **EBT 3 diamonds.** *"Elegant, spacious
licensed private hotel at the bottom of Beacon Hill, tea/coffee-
making facilities, colour TV. Library of tourist info."*

Penrith

Mrs Jackie Foster Voreda View, 2 Portland Place, Penrith, CA11 7QN

Telephone/Fax	**01768 863395 mobile 0410 409301**
Rooms	2 single + 3 twin + 3 double +1 family
B&B	£15.00-£19.50 Packed lunch £3.50
Distance from C2C	On route Pub nearby

AA QQ. *"Family owned Victorian guest house offering a warm and friendly welcome. Provides good, service, spacious accommodation and Sky Sports."*

Sylvia Jackson Norcroft Guest House,Graham Street Penrith, Cumbria CA11 9LQ

Telephone/Fax	**01768 862365**
Rooms	3 family + 2 double + 3 twin +1 single
B&B	£16.00-£21.00
Evening meal	£5.95 *(prior notice please)*
Packed Lunch	£3.50
Distance from C2C	On route Pub nearby

3 Diamonds Commended. *"Large Victorian house, comfortable rooms, mostly en-suite, tea/coffee-making facilities, colour TV, drying facilities, secure cycle storage."*
(See Advertisement on Page 81)

Mr Graham Carruthers Roundthorn Country House, Beacon Edge, Penrith, CA11 8SJ

Telephone	**01768 863952 Fax 01768 864100**
e-mail	**enquires@roundthorn.fsnet.co.uk**
Rooms	2 twin + 8 double +2 family
B&B	£25.00-£30.00 Packed lunch £3.00
Distance from C2C	On route Pub 1 mile

3 Diamonds *"A beautiful Georgian mansion with spectacular views. All rooms en-suite, licensed bar, washing and drying facilities and a hearty Cumbrian breakfast."*

Edenhall

The Proprietor	The Country Hotel, Edenhall,
	nr Penrith, Cumbria CA11 8SX
Telephone	**01768 881454** Fax 01768 881266
Rooms	4 double + 6 single + 10 twins
	4 family rooms *(all en-suite)*
B&B	£25.00
Evening meal	From £5.50 Packed lunch £3.95
Distance from C2C	On route Hotel has Public Bar

2 Star Hotel. *"Country house hotel in beautiful surroundings. TV, telephone, tea/coffee in all rooms. Excellent food. Secure cycle storage and drying facilities. Telephone for brochure."*

Langwathby

Mrs Karen Peet	Hayloft Bunkhouse, Langwathby Hall,
	Langwathby, nr Penrith, CA10 1LW
Telephone	**01768 881771** Fax 01768 881802
Rooms	36 bunks (2 cubicles of 8 + 2 of 10)
B&B	£13.00 (Full English)
Packed lunch	£3.50
Distance from C2C	On route Pub 150 yds

(No smoking please.) *"Very comfortable bunkhouse accommodation in converted stable loft, with hot showers, and breakfast served in the farmhouse. Eden Ostrich World."*

Clive Gravett	Langstanes, Culgaith Road,
	Langwathby, nr Penrith CA10 1NA
Telephone/Fax	**01768 881004**
Rooms	2 double + 1 twin *(all en-suite)*
B&B	£19.50 Packed lunch from £3.50
Distance from C2C	On route Pub 300 yds

(No smoking please.) **ETB 4 Diamonds** *"Comfortable sandstone house on route, tea/coffee-making facilities, colour TV, secure bike storage, drying facilities."*

Little Salkeld

The Proprietors	Bank House Farm and Stables, Little Salkeld, nr Penrith, Cumbria CA10 INN
Telephone/fax	**01768 881257**
Rooms	1 double + 1 family + 1 twin
B&B	£18.00-£20.00
Packed lunch	£3.50
Distance from C2C	On route
Pub	1 mile

"Great B&B. Enjoy a relaxing time in peaceful surroundings in our lovely old farmhouse. Home baked rolls and an Aga cooked breakfast."

Renwick

Mr and Mrs Milburn	Half Way Bunk House, Busk Rigg, Renwick, nr Penrith, Cumbria CA10 1LA *(£40.00 per bunk room)*
Telephone	**01768 898288 or 897155**
Rooms	2 rooms, 6 bunks each, £8.00 *(sleeping bags available-please phone)*
Evening meal	By arrangement Packed lunch £3.50
Distance from C2C	½ mile Pub 3½ miles

"Located in the hamlet of Busk on working farm. Kitchen with hob, microwave oven, toaster and fridge. Storage heating, shower, toilets, dining and sitting area - lift to pub available."

Melmerby

*This delightful village is 3 miles off the route but is well worth the visit as it has so much to offer and lots of facilities. The **Village Bakery** has a coffee shop and restaurant. It is famous for excellent home baking. The **Shepherds Inn** is renouned for its delicious puddings and its Egon Ronay Listing.*

Thomas and Margaret Frazer	Bolton Farmhouse, Melmerby, nr Penrith, Cumbria CA10 1HF
Telephone	**01768 881851 Mobile 0402 933 952**
Rooms	1 single + 1 double + 1 twin
B&B	£15.00 Distance from C2C 3 miles

"Clean, comfortable and friendly 18th-c village farmhouse, centrally situated, in an 'area of outstanding natural beauty'. All welcome. Worth a visit. Nearby pub serves good food."

Mrs Ann Comb	Post Haste, Melmerby, nr Penrith, Cumbria CA10 1HF
Telephone	**01768 881251**
Rooms	1 double + 1 family room
B&B	From £15.00-£18.00
Distance from C2C	3 miles
Pub	Next door

"Situated at village store. Family room has kitchen allowing for either B&B or self-catering. Dining room features log fire in old fashioned range."

Mrs Edith James	Greenholme, Melmerby, nr Penrith, Cumbria CA10 1HB
Telephone	**01768 881436**
Web	www.erudite.co.uk/greenholme
Rooms	1 double + 1 double with extra bed + 1 double with extra bed en-suite
B&B	From £18.00-£20.00
Distance from C2C 3 miles	Pub nearby

(No smoking please.) "Comfortable accommodation for the weary cyclist. All rooms have tea/coffee-making facilities. A good English break-fast before the big climb up Hartside."

ALSTON

Market Square

A picture postcard Cumbrian market town hidden away in England's last wilderness. Cobbled streets wind steeply up to the old market square where you will find quaint old cafés and shops. This historic town, built on the confluence of the South Tyne and the river Nent, owes much to the lead-mining heritage of the area. The mines and their machinery are silent now, but scattered hill farms where mining families grew crops to subsidise their meagre wages and the haunting sound of the curlew still remain. Once you visit this area, its beauty and history will lure you back to explore more of its secrets.

South Tynedale Railway

Alston Tourist Information

PLACES OF INTEREST

Hartside Nursery Garden On route 1 mile from Alston: rare and unusual alpine plants

South Tynedale Railway TIC and beautifully restored Victorian station, England's highest narrow-gauge railway 01434 381696

EATING OUT

Gossipgate Gallery The Butts, back of the old market: tea room and craft gallery 01434 381806

The Angel Town Centre 01434 381363

Lowbyer Manor Excellent food - Main course £16.50 Mrs Hughes 01434 381230

C2C Route Features: *the route does not officially go through Alston. It goes to Leadgate and thence to Garrigill and Nenthead. Garrigill has a post office and pub. Nenthead has a newly opened* **Mines Heritage Centre,** *a pub, a cafè and village shop. If you take the Stanhope route, Killhope Lead-mining Centre is excellent.*

WARNING! This area is in a very remote corner of the UK: places to buy food or stay over-night are few and far between.

Alston Moor

Leadgate

Mike and Clare Le Marie	Brownside House, Leadgate, Alston, Cumbria CA9 3EL
Telephone	**Fax/phone 01434 382169**
	Phone 01434 382100
e-mail	brownside_hse@hotmail.com
Rooms	1 double + 2 twin + 1 single
B&B	£18.00
Evening meal	£6.50 Packed lunch £2.50
Distance from C2C	On route Pub 2 miles

3 Diamonds *"Quiet, peaceful situation in the country with a warm welcome. Home cooking, hot bath. Residents' lounge with TV and log fire. Secure storage for bikes."*

Alston

Mr and Mrs P.J. & M. Hughes	Lowbyer Manor Country House Hotel, Alston, Cumbria CA9 3JX
Telephone	**01434 381230** Fax 01434 382937
Rooms	6 double + 2 single + 4 twins
B&B	£29.50 *(all rooms en-suite)*
Dinner (à la carte)	From £10.50Packed lunch from £3.50
Distance from C2C	On alternative route Pub nearby

2 Star Hotel *"Family-run 17th-c manor, substantial breakfast & a la carte dinner. In quiet wooded location on edge of Alston. Drying facilities available. Secure garage for bikes."*

Mrs Jean Best	Chapel House B&B, Alston, Cumbria CA9 3SH Telephone **01434 381112**
Rooms	1 double + 1 single + 1 twin + 1 family
B&B	£15.00-£17.00
Evening meal	£8.00 *(prior notice please)*
Packed lunch	£3.00
Distance from C2C	On alternative route Pub nearby

(No smoking in some areas please.) **3 diamonds** *"17th-c Chapel, a friendly welcome to clean, comfortable accommodation and good home-cooking."*

Alston

Adam Ferguson   St Paul's Mission, Town Head, Alston,
                    Cumbria CA9 3SL
Telephone/Fax   **01434 382441**
Rooms   36 bed-cubicled accommodation
B&B   £10.00-£15.00
Distance from C2C   On alternative route Pub nearby
(No smoking please.) *"100 yds from Market Square, 8 show-
ers and W.C.s, indoor bike security, sauna, large lounge,
Sky TV, cooking , launderette, full central heating, large gar-
den."* **(Please see advertisement on page 82.)**

Mrs Coleman   Albert House Guesthouse,Townhead,
                    Alston, Cumbria CA9 3SL
Telephone/fax   **01434 381793**
Rooms   2 double + 2 twin + 2 family
B&B   £20.00
Evening meal   £6.00-£12.00   Packed lunch £3.50
Distance from C2C   On alternative route Pub nearby
*(No smoking please.)***ETB 3 diamonds** *"After a hard day in
the saddle enjoy the luxury of Albert House. Warm and
friendly. Excellent evening meals. Large Cumbrian breakfast
and substantial packed lunches."*

Mrs Pat Dent   Greycroft, Middle Park, The Raise,
                    Alston,Cumbria CA9 3JH
Telephone   **01434 381383**
Rooms   1 double + 1 family *(all en suite)*
B&B   £18.00-£20.00 Ev. meal from £10.00
Distance from C2C   On alternative route Pub 3/4 mile
4 Diamonds *"After 25 years of farmhouse B&B at Garrigil
come and enjoy our new home, furnished to a high standard,
centrally heated rooms, all home cooking. A warm welcome to
all."*

45

GARRIGILL

This peaceful little village was once a bustling lead mining community. In 1831 the population was 1,614, today it is a mere 225. The rounded hillocks around the village betray the site of lead mine workings, many of them tree covered, but in the mining heyday not a tree was to be seen between Nenthead and Alston.

The surrounding hillsides are a honeycomb of mining tunnels. When times were hard for the miners they would turn their skills to poaching the local game. A pheasant or hare poached from the local gentry was a welcome feast for a hungry mining family. At one time the King's Hussars were called in to restrain the poachers, but the men of Garrigill knew where to hide!

Poachers!

Garrigill has a Pub and a Post Office, and some guest-houses do excellent evening meals.

Garrigill

Mrs Pauline Platts High Windy Hall Hotel & Restaurant,
(on B6277)   Above Garrigill, Alston, CA9 3EZ
Telephone   **01434 381547**
Fax   **01434 382477**
e-mail   sales@hwh.u-net.com
Web site   www.hwh.u-net.com
Rooms   2 double+1 twin+2 family *(all en-suite)*
B&B   £26.00-£35.00
Evening meal   From £20.00
Packed lunch   £3.50
Distance from C2C 200 metres
Pub   ½ mile

(No smoking in bedrooms please.) **ETB 2 diamonds.** *"Family-run licensed hotel, good food, interesting wine list, peaceful views overlooking South Tyne Valley, well-deserved luxury after Hartside Pass."*

Lead Mining

Garrigill

Anne Bramwell   Post Office Guest House, Garrigill, Alston, Cumbria CA9 3DS

Telephone   **01434 381257/Fax 01434 381257**
Rooms   1 double + 2 twin + 2 singles
B&B   £16.00   Packed lunch £3.50
Distance from C2C On route   Pub nearby

(No smoking please.) "*The Post Office is a 300 year old house. Tea/coffee-making facilities, radio alarms and hair dryers in all rooms, separate residents' lounge with TV. Drying facilities available. Good food at pub next door.*"

Laurie Humble   Ivy House, Garrigill, CA9 3DU
Telephone/Fax   **01434 382501/Fax01434 382660**
e-mail   ivyhousebb@aol.com
Rooms   3 double/twin + 2 family *(all en-suite)*
                   3 singles -*Three rooms in total*
B&B   £17.00-£29.00
Evening meal   £8.00-£15.00
Packed lunch   £4.00
Distance from C2C On route
Pub   nearby

(No smoking please.) **4 Diamonds**
"*Converted 17th-c farmhouse. Comfortable en-suite rooms with TVs. Cycle storage/cleaning/re-pair/hire/baggage & transfer facilities. Laundry service. CTC affiliated. Friendly fellow - cycling hosts!*".

NENTHEAD

Nenthead from Garrigill Road

Nestling in the bowl of its surrounding hills, Nenthead is one of the highest villages in England. It was the most important lead-mining centre in the North Pennines from the beginning of 18th-c. Lead was probably discovered very early by accident when local farmers used fire to crack the stone in order to build walls around their land. It was found that a substance in the rock melted and could be formed into useful vessels. Much later they realised that the lead had great commercial value and small drift mines were opened.

The Quaker born London Lead Mining Company contributed enormously to the welfare of all the local inhabitants as well as the miners. The Company gradually provided Nenthead with all the social services such as schools, chapels, shops, a reading room, village hall and houses. The 'Miners Arms' regularly had its rent reduced as trade diminished due to the miners "preferring books to beer"! Obviously the Quaker influence was a healthy one!

Nenthead Tourist Information

PLACES OF INTEREST

Mines Heritage Centre Excellent visitor centre with refreshments and Bunk House

EATING OUT

The Crown Inn Has a paddock at back for campers (please put donation in box!)
01434 381271

The Miners Arms Bunk House 01434 381427

Mines Heritage Centre Café 01434 382037

BIKE REPAIRS

Mark Fearn Blacksmith - repairs bikes & carries some spares. Phone **01434 382194**
Bike & rider recovery where possible

Carting lead

Nenthead

Hope Alderson Mill Cottage Bunkhouse, Nenthead, Alston, Cumbria CA9 3PD
Telephone **01434 382726** Fax 382294
Bunkhouse Sleeps 9 Bed only £8.00
B&B £12.00 Packed lunch £3.50
Distance from C2C On route Pub nearby

"Superior quality bunkhouse accommodation. Right on C2C route. Set amidst spectacular scenery. Washing/drying facilities. Fully fitted kitchen. Secure cycle storage."

Mrs Hellen Sherlock Cherry Tree, Nenthead, Alston, Cumbria CA9 3PD
Telephone **01434 381434** or **01434 382368**
Rooms 2 double + 2 family + 1 single
B&B £15.00 Packed lunch £3.00
Distance from C2C 200 yards Pubs nearby

"Stonebuilt farmhouse in pleasant surroundings. 2 bathrooms with electric showers and individual shower rooms, full central heating. Secure lock-up for bikes."

The Miners Arms Nenthead, Alston, Cumbria CA9 3PF
Telephone **01434 381427**
e-mail miners.arms@talk21.com
Rooms 2 double, 2 family, 2 twin, 2 single
B&B £15.00
Bunkhouse Sleeps 12 B&B £10.00
Evening meals From £4.00 Packed lunch £3.25
Distance from C2C On route Stamping Post

(No smoking in bedrooms or bunkhouse please.) "Friendly family pub offering homely accommodation.National prize-winning menu. Home-made food and real ale. Bike spares available."

ALLENHEADS

Allenheads, reputed to be England's highest village, would have looked very different 100 years ago. A valley filled with toneless grey slag heaps and shrouded by the smog from miners' cottage fires would have greeted you. Today this friendly little hamlet, almost hidden in pine trees, welcomes you off the moor with its babbling beck and good places to eat and rest. Allenheads once supplied a sixth of Britain's lead until cheap foreign imports brought tumbling prices and an end to the village's mining prosperity.

PLACES OF INTEREST

Heritage Centre	In the midst of the village.
Old School House	Art Exhibitions.
Old Blacksmith's Shop	Displays of local items.

PLACES TO EAT

The Henmel Café	Welcoming oasis for the tired, wet and hungry cyclist.
Old School House	Fresh, delicious hearty home cooking
The Village Shop	Has a good supply of food as well as basic essentials for your bike.

Allenheads

Peter & Linda Stenson The Allenheads Inn, Allenheads, Hexham, Northumberland NE47 9HJ

Telephone/Fax **01434 685200**

Rooms 3 double + 4 twin + 1 family *(en-suite)* (cottage for groups)

B&B £21.50-£25.00

Evening meal From £4.75

Distance from C2C On route Pub

"Its the place they all talk about. Eccentric and entertaining, warm & comfortable. En-suite accommodation. Well kept beers and tasty food." **(See advertisement on page 83)**

Helen Ratcliffe and Alan Smith The Old School House, Allenheads, Northumberland NE47 9HR

Telephone/Fax **01434 685040**

e-mail headalan@aol.com

Rooms 1 family room (sleeps 1-4) + 1 spacious room for larger groups

B&B £15.00-£17.00

Evening meal Available

Distance from C2C On route Pub nearby

"A friendly, colourful and interesting place. Superb dinner and tremendous breakfast, best so far on route. Great atmosphere, unrivalled views. Altogether a wonderful place to stay!" (Quotes from C2C'ers)

The Allenheads Trust, Allenheads Heritage Centre, Allenheads Northumberland NE47 9UQ. Telephone **01434 685374**. *Fax 0191 514 4947(Advertisement on page 85)*

Allenheads

Allenheads Lodge Outdoor Centre, Allenheads Village, Northumberland NE47 9HW. Telephone/Fax **01434 685374.** 22 beds in 4 dormitory bedrooms. Breakfast, evening meals and self-catering options available. Large groups welcome. Back-up transport + full C2C package on request. Prices start from £8.25 pp pn. On C2C route. Pub nearby. *(No smoking in bedrooms please.)*

Morris Muter	Spring House, Allenheads,
	Hexham, Northumberland NE47 9HJ
Telephone/Fax	**01434 685301**
Rooms	2 twins + 2 family *(en-suite)*
	(cottage for groups)
B&B	£17.50-£20.00
Evening meal	From £5.00-£12.00 Pk. Lunch £3.50
Distance from C2C	On route Pub

*"Spring house is situated 300 ft above Allenheads village. Panoramic views can be enjoyed from the house. Comfortable rooms. Lounge with TV and wood-burning stove."***(See advertisement on page 85.)**

ROOKHOPE

This little-visited settlement welcomes you after a glorious two miles free-wheel ride from the last summit. Rookhope keeps the secret of its hiding place well guarded as it nestles far from sight high above the Weardale Valley. It is hard to imagine that this small group of dwellings was a hive of

activity only a few years ago. In its heyday it supported a surgery, a resident district nurse, vicar, policeman, teashops, several crowded pubs and a busy school. The mining of lead, iron and fluorspar, smelting and railways totally dominated people's lives with clockwork regularity. Today the village is a welcome watering hole and resting place for weary cyclists before the final leg of the C2C journey down to the NE coast.

There is an information centre at Rookhope Nurseries, and a pub, village shop and several guest-houses.

Rookhope

Lintzgarth Arch

Lintzgarth Arch stands enormous, abandoned and out of place on the valley floor on the approach to Rookhope. The arch carried a horizontal chimney across the valley which replaced the more conventional vertical type when it was realised that a lot of lead literally went up with the smoke. Consequently young chimney sweeps were employed to scrape the valuable lead and silver deposits from the chimney once a week. A dangerous job done by youngsters long before the days of Health and Safety!

Broken flue and chimney

Rookhope

Mike and Kay Leathers Garden Cottage Guest House, 7 Front Street, Rookhope, Bishop Auckland DL13 2AZ

Telephone **01388 517577**
Rooms 1 double + 1 twin + 1 family + 1 single
B&B £16.00
Evening meal £6.00 Packed lunch £3.50
Distance from C2C On route Pub nearby

(No smoking in bedrooms please.) "Stone-built cottage with beamed ceilings, open fires, guests' lounge, TV and tea/coffee in bedrooms, 4 bathrooms (one with a Jacuzzi), drying facilities, garage for bikes. Great food, warm welcome."

Janette and Tony Newbon High Brandon, Rookhope, Weardale, Co. Durham, DL13 2AF

Telephone **01388 517673**
e-mail **newbon@highbrandonbb.fsbusiness.co.uk**
Rooms 1 single + 1 twin + 1 family
B&B From £17.00
Evening Meal £5.00-£12.00 Packed lunch £2.50
Distance from C2C On route Pub 1 mile

(No smoking please.) "A superior farmhouse B&B. Open fires, exposed beams, warm and very atmospheric. Excellent food & accommodation. A superb welcome for weary cylists."
4 diamonds

Rookhope

Colin & Pauline Lomas

The Old Vicarage, Rookhope in Weardale, Co. Durham, DL13 2AF

Telephone/fax	**01388 517375**
Rooms	1 single + 1 double
B&B	£17.50
Evening Meal	£7.50 Packed lunch £3.50
Distance from C2C	On route Pub *(lift available)*

(Large detatched, stone built house in own secluded grounds. Spacious room with tea and coffee making facilities. TV + video, garage for bikes and drying facilities. Resident dog. Camping in the garden available.

Breaking and washing iron-ore

STANHOPE

You may wish to cycle via Stanhope, an attractive Weardale village nestling between the Northern Dales. The village expanded in 1845 when the Stanhope & Tyne Railway was constructed. A standing engine hauled the heavy wagons up Crawley Side. It then continued on its journey down the Waskerley Way to Consett and Cleveland.

PLACES OF INTEREST

Dales Visitor Centre	Town centre 01388 527650
	Good cafe too.
Fossil tree at St Thomas's Church	350 million years old, found in 1914 in an Edmundbyers mine
EATING OUT	
Stanhope Old Hall	A la carte menu 01388 528 451
Various pubs	All in town centre
CYCLE SHOPS	
Weardale Mountain Bikes	Frosterley 01388 528129 (within 5 miles of C2C)

*C2C Features: the route leads you up Crawley Side, aptly named due to its steep incline, and on up to the **Waskerley Way**. Before the railways were built, all raw materials were transported by pack horses. Teams of tough little Galloway horses would pick their way across the wind-swept Pennines and then down into the valleys. The lead horse often had a bell attached to his harness to guide the following horses across the mist-cloaked moors.*

Stanhope

Mrs. Storey   Queen's Head Hotel, 89 Front Street,
                  Stanhope, Weardale DL13 2UB
Telephone   **01388 528160**
Rooms   4 twins
B&B   £18.00
Evening meal   From £3.00
Packed lunch   £3.00
Distance from C2C   c. 1 mile   Hotel has Public Bar

"Small family-run country pub, full licence, fine real ales. All rooms have colour TV and tea/coffee-making facilities."

Mrs E. Hamilton   Red Lodge Guest House, 2 Market
                      Place, Stanhope, DL13 2UN
Telephone   **01388 527851**
e-mail   redlodge@netline.uk.net
Rooms   1 double + 1 twin + 1 family +1 single
B&B   £18.00-£20.00
Distance from C2C   c.1 mile   Pub nearby

"Family run guest-house, well-equipped with TV and tea/coffee-making facilities in all rooms. Pubs and fast food take-aways nearby. Quote from visitor's book 1999 - 'Weary cyclist's rating - Bed 5 Star, Welcome 5 Star & Food 5 Star!' "

CONSETT

As the C2C approaches Consett it passes the site of the Old Consett Steel Works which originally opened in 1837. It was eventually closed and the enormous site was dismantled in 1980. This ghost-like empty space of 700 acres now looks strange and desolate after those Dickensian years when the night skies glowed bright with fires from hungry steel blast-furnaces.

PLACES OF INTEREST

Phileas Fogg Factory   Alias Derwent Valley Foods

Shotley Bridge   An old spa town, well-known for German sword-makers in the 17th-c

EATING OUT

Grey Horse   Real Ales brewed on the premises! Light lunches and right on C2C route.

Jolly Drovers Pub   Leadgate 01207 503 994

CYCLE SHOPS

Consett Cycle Co   62 Medomsley Rd 01207 581 205

McVickers Sports   Front Street 01207 505 121

C2C Features: dotted along the line are story-boards set on vertical sleepers which interpret the history of the railway. These are chapters taken from a novel, The Celestial Railroad, *by John Downie. It is available from Sustrans North Eastern Office at Stanley, 01207 281259.*

Castleside

Liz Lawson Bee Cottage Farm, Castleside,
Consett, Co. Durham DH8 9HW

Telephone **01207 508224**
Rooms 5 double + 6 family + 1 single
B&B From £22.00 On C2C route
Evening meal £14.50 Packed lunch £4.50

(No smoking please.) **ETB 2 Crowns Highly Commended.**
*"Working farm with lovely views, situated close to the Waskerley Way (between points 105 and 106 on C2C map). Sleeps 34. Warm welcome, home comforts, **good food and plenty of it**! Tearoom open 1pm-6pm all summer." (**See Page 84.**)*

Noel and Jane Castleside Inn, Staniford-Dam, Consett,
Reid Co. Durham DH8 8EP

Telephone **01207 581443** Fax 01207 583373
Internet http://www.scoot.co.uk/castleside
Rooms 1 single + 4 double + 2 twin + 1 family
B&B £17.95-£26.95 *(10% discount for C2C)*
Meals available 11.00am-10.30pm Public Bar
Packed lunch Available On C2C Route

*"Rural setting very near C2C route. Carry on over A68. Turn left after viaduct by old coal wagon! Quality accommodation, all en-suite." (**See advertisement on page 86.**)*

Consett

Alex Forsyth Consett YMCA, Parliament Street,
Consett, Co. Durham DH8 5DH

Telephone **01207 502680** Fax **01207 501578**
Rooms 12 family rooms Pub nearby
B&B £12.50 Evening meal £5.00
Distance from C2C Very near Packed lunch £3.00

*"We have a drying room, workshop for repairs, a conservatory, colour TV, bar and lounge, table tennis and pool table, roller-blade disco and a gym if you have the energy left!" (**See advertisement on page 83.**)*

STANLEY

*Stanley is set on a breezy hill top and commands a bird's eye view of the whole area. **Sustrans North Eastern Office** is at Rockwood House, Barn Hill, Stanley, Co. Durham DH9 8AN. Tel: 01207 281259, Fax 01207 281113. Information on other Sustrans Bike Routes is available here together with interesting booklets and C2C T-shirts. You may join the Sustrans Charity here. They are responsible for creating a UK cycleway network.*

PLACES OF INTEREST

Tanfield Railway	World's oldest operating railway!
Beamish	Open-air museum

EATING OUT

Hill Top Restaurant	East Street 01207 233217
Asda	On ring road, Coffee Shop
Shafto's Bar	Causey Farm 01207 235555

CYCLE SHOPS

Main Brothers	Front Street 01207 290258

C2C Features: Beamish Museum is England's largest open-air museum and has a working steam railway, trams, a Victorian town centre, a demonstration colliery, a school and a working farm. The C2C route passes within yards of the entrance gate.

Stanley

Mrs Pamela Gibson	Bushblades Farm, Harperley, nr Stanley, Co. Durham DH9 9UA
Telephone	**01207 232722**
Rooms	2 double + 1 twin
B&B	£17.00-£19.50
Distance from C2C	½ mile
Pub	½ mile

(Smoking in bedrooms only please.)
ETB Listed, Commended, AA QQ.
"Comfortable Georgian farmhouse with large garden in rural setting. En-suite available. Colour TV tea/ coffee facilities in all rooms. Close to Beamish Museum."

Beamish

Clare Jones	Beamish Mary Inn, No Place, Beamish, Co. Durham DH9 0QH
Telephone	**0191 370 0237** Fax 0191 370 0091
Rooms	2 double + 1 family *(all en-suite)*
B&B	£17.50-£21.00
Evening meal	From £4.00
Packed lunch	From £2.50
Distance from C2C	¼ mile
Pub	Nearby

3 Diamonds *"Traditional Inn. Specialises in good food, real ale, live music. Comfortable atmosphere. All rooms en-suite, 1 with bath. (Landlord and landlady both keen cyclists.)"*

CHESTER-LE-STREET

Chester-le-Street is the oldest town in County Durham, and was once a Roman settlement. The Washington Wildfowl and Wetlands Centre is very near the route. This 100-acre waterfowl park designed by Peter Scott has over 1,200 birds and is visited by several mammals including the scarce water vole.

PLACES OF INTEREST

The Washington   100 acres of magnificent parkland, ponds
Wetlands Trust   and hides 0191 416 5454

EATING OUT

The Wheatsheaf   Pelaw Grange 0191 388 3104
The Barley Mow   Browns Buildings 0191 410 4504

CYCLE SHOPS

Cestria Cycles   11 Ashfield Terrace - 0191 388 7535

C2C Features: the Penshaw Monument, a look-alike Doric Temple dedicated to Theseus, was built in memory of John George Lambton, the 1st Earl of Durham. Be thankful to leave the river here for fear of the **Lambton Worm.** The legend runs that a young Lambton lad, fishing in the river against all advice, caught a small worm. In disgust he threw it into a nearby well and went off to fight in the Crusades. On his return the "worm" had grown into a dragon which ravaged the countryside. A witch agreed to slay the beast on condition that Lambton kill the first living thing he met. Unfortunately it was his father, whom of course he spared, and so failed to fulfil his side of the bargain, thus nine generations of Lambtons were condemned to meet untimely ends!

Chester-le-Street

Lambton Worm Hotel	52 North Road, Chester-le-Street, Co. Durham DH3 4AT
Telephone	**0191 388 3386**
Rooms	9 double + 4 single
B&B	£16.00-£28.00
Evening meals	£2.50-£15.00
Packed lunch	£3.50
Distance from C2C	On route Hotel has Public Bar

ETB 2 Crowns. *"13-bedroomed hotel/pub boasting 2 bars, excellent food, pool, darts, big-screen football. Tolerant understanding staff of muddy and exhausted bikers!"*

Beamish Open Air Museum

SUNDERLAND

Sunderland, once home of shipbuilding, coal-mining and glass making, became a city in 1992 and is just a stone's throw from the coast and the North Sea. **St Peter's Church**, *built in 674 when Sunderland became established as one of England's earliest centres of Christianity, was notable as the first "glazed" building in England.   George Washington's ancestral home is in* **Washington village,** *which is now part of the city of Sunderland: what an amazing connection with Whitehaven, the start of the C2C, where Washington's grandparents had their home!*

PLACES OF INTEREST

Washington Old Hall	In Washington village. George Washington's ancestral home 0191 416 6879
National Glass Centre	Demonstration of glass blowing & Throwing Stones Restaurant
Crowtree Leisure Centre	Town centre: have a celebratory swim - the sea could be a bit chilly! 0191 553 2600

EATING OUT

Marine Activity Centre	Trattoria Duo 0191 5100 600
Snow Goose Café	Good food & fun 0191 529 4091

CYCLE SHOPS

Peter Darke Cycles	113 High St West 0191 510 8155

For tourist and accommodation information on Newcastle, Tynemouth and Whitley Bay please turn to pages 96 - 99

Sunderland

Mrs Eileen Hughes
Brendon House, 49 Roker Park Road, Roker, Sunderland SR6 9PL

Telephone	**0191 548 9303**
e-mail	bredonhouse@hotmail.com
Rooms	3 double + 4 family + 1 single
B&B	£15.00-£18.00
Evening meal	£5.75 Packed lunch £3.25
Distance from C2C	½ mile Pub nearby

1 Crown Approved. *"5 minutes from Marine Centre and Railway Station. Clean, comfortable, spacious rooms with TV, tea/coffee making facilities. Ideal for weary travellers. Reductions for children. Bike storage."*

Karen & Robin Dawson
Belmont Guest House, 8 St Georges Terrace, Roker, Sunderland SR6 9LX

Telephone	**0191 567 2438 or 0191 5140689**
Rooms	10 double + 2 single
B&B	£18.00-£30.00
Distance from C2C	On route Pub nearby

ETB 2 Crowns. *"Small family-run guest-house. 100 yds from sea front and C2C route. En-suite rooms. Lock-up available for bikes. Warm welcome at the end of your ride."*

Camping & Caravan Sites

Workington/Whitehaven

Inglenook Caravan & Camping Park, Fitz Bridge, Lamplugh, Workington, CA14 4SH *(on C2C)* Tel/Fax **01946 861240**

Braithwaite

Scotgate Chalet, Camping & Caravan Holiday Park, Braithwaite, Keswick, Cumbria CA12 5TF *(C2C 100 yds)* Tel **017687 78343** *Fax 017687 78099*
(See advertisement page 78.)

Troutbeck

Gill Head Farm, Troutbeck, Penrith, Cumbria CA11 0ST Tel **017687 79652** *(See advertisement page 77.)*

Penruddock

Beckses Caravan & Camping Park, Penruddock, Penrith, Cumbria CA11 0RX *(c. ½ mile from C2C)*
Tel **017684 83224**

Alston

Horse & Waggon Camping & Caravan Park, Nentsberry, Alston, Cumbria CA9 3LH, William Patterson *(swings on play area, WC and showers available, 3 miles south-east Alston on A689. Tents from £4.00, OS map ref NY 764 451)*
Tel **01434 382805**

Rookhope

The Old Vicarage, Rookhope, Co Durham DL13 2AE
Tel 01388 517375

Hamsterley

Byreside Caravan Site, Hamsterley, Newcastle-upon-Tyne NE17 7RT, Mrs Val Clemitson *(between Ebchester and Hamsterley Mill, adjacent to Derwent Walk & Cycle Track)*
 Tel **01207 560280/560499**

Camping & Caravans Sites

Rowlands Gill

Derwent Park Caravan & Camping Site, Rowlands Gill, Tyne & Wear NE39 1LG. David Johnson *(discount for C2C cyclists. 100m from C2C Route)*

Tel/Fax **01207 543383 (see advertisement on page 88)**

Beamish

Bobby Shafto Caravan Park, Beamish, Co. Durham DH9 0RY *(adjacent to world famous Beamish Museum, only ¾ mile from C2C route)*

Tel **0191 370 1776** Fax 0191 456 1083

Bunk Houses

Penrith	Corney House. MrsMawer 01768 **867627**
Langwathby	The Hayloft. Mrs Peet **01768 881661**
Renwick	Half Way Bunkhouse, Busk Rigg Farm, Mrs Milburn **01768 898288**
Alston	St Paul's Mission, Townhead. **01434 382441**
Nenthead	Heritage Centre. **01434 382726**
	Miners Arms. **01434 381427**

Youth Hostels

YHA, Northern Region, PO Box 11, Matlock, Derbyshire DE4 2XA (inc SAE)

Tel **01629 825850** *(See advertisement page 88)*

Cockermouth Youth Hostel

Double Mills, Cockermouth, Cumbria CA13 0DS
£4.95 (under 18's) £7.20 (adults) + Breakfast £2.95 Evening meal £4.40 *(on C2C route)*

Tel **01900 822561**

Skiddaw House Youth Hostel

Bassenthwaite, Keswick, Cumbria CA12 4QX
£3.85 (under 18's) £5.65 (adults), self-catering only

Tel **016974 78325**

Keswick Youth Hostel

Station Road, Keswick, Cumbria CA12 5LH
£6.55 (under 18s) £9.75 (adults) + Breakfast £2.95 *Membership requirement: available at Hostel. (on C2C route)*
Tel **017687 72484**

Alston Youth Hostel

The Firs, Alston, Cumbria CA9 3RW £5.40 (under 18s) £8.00 (adults) + Breakfast £2.95 *(2 miles from C2C route)*
Tel **01434 381509** Fax 01434 382401

Edmundbyers Youth Hostel

Low House, Edmundbyers, Consett, Co Durham DH8 9NL £4.45 (under 18s) £6.50 (adults), self-catering only *(on C2C route)* Tel/Fax **01207 255651**

Consett YMCA

Parliament Street, Consett, Co. Durham DH8 5DH 12 rooms, 65 beds in Alpine style rooms. B&B £12.50. Evening meal £5.00. Packed lunch £3.00. OS Ref. 105 509. ***(See advertisement page 89.)*** Tel **01207 502680** Fax 01207 501578

Newcastle upon Tyne Youth Hostel

107 Jesmond Road, Newcastle upon Tyne NE2 1NJ
£5.15 (under 18s) £7.70 (adults) + Breakfast £2.85
Tel **0191 281 2570**

Camping Barns

Camping Barns are stone barns providing simple overnight shelter. They are roomy and dry, so there is no need to carry a tent. They have a wooden sleeping platform sometimes with mattresses. Tables, a slate cooking bench and cold water tap and WC are also provided together with a washing-up bowl, clothes hooks and waste bags.

Cumbria: for bookings at most of the Lake District National Park barns you must first ring Keswick Information Centre on **017687 72803**

Loweswater - Swallow Barn, Waterend Farm *(west end of Loweswater, on C2C route)* OS NY 116 226
Newlands Valley - Catbells Barn, *(c. 2 miles from C2C route)* OS NY 243 208
Keswick - Eagle's Nest Barn, Low Grove Farm, Millbeck, *(c. 2 miles from C2C route)* OS NY 258 259
Mungrisdale - Blake Beck Barn between Keswick and Penrith, *(c. 2 miles from C2C route)* OS NY 367 278
Renwick Half Way Bunk House. Phone **01768 898288**
Alston - Wearhead Camping Barn, Black Cleugh, Cowshill, Wearhead, Co. Durham DL13 1DJ *(c. 2 miles from C2C route)* Tel **01388 537 395** Mr Robert Walton OS NY 436 821

Useful Telephone Numbers

Weather News

Cumbria & the Lake District Weathercall	0891 500 419
North East England Weathercall	0891 500 418

Tourist Information Centres

Whitehaven	01946 852939
Keswick	017687 72645
Cockermouth	01900 822634
Penrith	01768 867466
Alston (April to October)	01434 381696
Stanhope	01388 527650
Beamish	0191 370 2533
Gateshead	0191 477 3478
Sunderland	0191 553 2000
Newcastle upon Tyne	0191 261 0610
Whitley Bay	0191 200 8535

Travel Information: Bus, Coach and Train

Stagecoach Cumberland	01946 63222
Cumbria County Council Travellink	01228 606000
Durham County Council Travellink	0191 383 3337
Tyne & Wear County Council Travellink	0191 232 5325
National Express	0990 808080
National Express Newcastle	0191 232 3300
National Rail Enquiries Line	0345 484 950
Scotrail Enquiries Line	0345 550 033
Cycle Booking Line NW Trains	0845 6040231

Bike Shops and Repairs

Whitehaven	Kershaw's Cycles, 125 Queen St 01946 590700
	Mark Taylor Cycles, 5/6 New St 01946 692252
Workington	Traffic Lights Bikes, 35 Washington St 01900 603283
	New Bike Shop, 18-20 Market Pl 01900 603337
Cockermouth	Wordsworth Hotel Bike Hire 01900 822757
	Derwent Cycles, 4 Market Place 01900 822113
Braithwaite	The Stores 017687 78273
Keswick	Keswick Mountain Bikes, Southey Hill 017687 75202
	Glaramara Guest House 017687 73216 (P.00)
Penrith	Arragons, 2 Brunswick Rd 01768 890344
	Harpers, 1-2 Middlegate 01768 864475
Alston	Nentholme B&B, The Butts 01434 381 523
Garrigil	Chris Humble, Ivy Farmhouse 01434 382501
Nenthead	Mark Fearn, blacksmith 01434 382194
Allenheads	Village Shop: essential bike spares
Stanhope	Weardale Mountain Bikes, Frosterley 01388 528129
Consett	Consett Cycle Co, 62 Medomsley Rd 01207 581 205
	McVickers Sports, Front St 01207 505 121
Stanley	Main Brothers, Front St 01207 290 258
Chester-le-St	Cestria Cycles, 11 Ashfield Terr 0191 3887535
Washington	Bike Shed, 3 Westview, Concord 0191 416 906
	Bike Rack, 65-66 In Shops 0191 419 1521
Metro Centre	The Bike Place, 8 Allison Court 0191 488 3137
Newcastle	Newcastle Cycle Centre, 165 Westgate Rd 0191 230 3022
Byker	Hardisty Cycles, 5 Union Rd 0191 265 8619
Sunderland	Darke Cycles, 113 High St W 0191 510 8155
	Cycle World, 118 High St West 0191 565 8188
Tynemouth	Cyclepath, 4 Queensway, 0191 258 6600

C2C Check List

Tool Kit

Chain splitter
Pump
Allen keys
Adjustable spanner
Screwdriver
Tyre levers
Spoke key
Strong tape (for quick repairs)
Chain & gear lubricant

Bike Spares

Puncture repair kit
Front and rear lights
Batteries
Spare chain links
Brake blocks
Straddle wire
Bike lock
Inner tube

Personal Kit

Wash kit
Money / credit card
Head torch
First aid kit
Liners for bags
Emergency rations
Water bottle
Survival bag
One change of cloths
Map & B&B Guide

Clothing

Towel
Cycle shorts (padded)
Cycle shirt/fleece top
Thermal vest
Helmet
Gloves
Fleece
Windproof top
Waterproof jacket
Waterproof trousers
Boots/shoes/trainers
Track suit bottoms
Underwear
3 pairs socks

Morven House Hotel
Siddick Road
Workington
Cumbria
CA14 1LE
Tel/Fax 01900 602118

Relaxed and informal atmosphere for guests. En-suite rooms. Good food. Ideal stop over for C2C participants. Start your tour in comfortable, detached house with car park and secure cycle storage. You may leave your car until your return if you wish.

English Tourist Board

RAC
HIGHLY
ACCLAIMED

"Take nothing but photographs
Leave nothing but tyre-tracks"

Glenlea House, Whitehaven

Don't miss the opportunity to sit on our terrace with an evening drink and enjoy magnificent views stretching as far as the eye can see from the harbour to the Isle of Man. We will take care of your car while you are away.

Mrs Oliver, Glenlea House, Lowca, Whitehaven, Cumbria CA28 6PS Tel 01946 693873 Fax 01946 694350

Gill Head Farm

Mrs J. Wilson
Gill Head Farm
Troutbeck
Penrith
Cumbria CA11 0ST
Tel 017687 79652

Bed and Breakfast + Camping. Stay in the comfortable 17th-century farmhouse with oak beams and log fires. Enjoy traditional home-cooking. All rooms are en-suite, with tea/coffee-making facilities, colour TV, and central heating throughout. For campers we have a level, sheltered campsite, with laundry and shop. The Troutbeck Inn is a 5 minute walk - bike no further!

SCOTGATE
Chalet, Camping & Caravan
HOLIDAY PARK

Chalets, Camping & Caravans
HOLIDAY PARK
Proprietors: Stuart Bros.
Peacefully situated between Bassenthwaite Lake
and Derwentwater with easy access
to all areas of Lakeland

CARAVANS & CHALETS TO LET
Fully Equipped - Toilet - Shower - Colour Television
Chalets also have videos and microwaves

SITE FOR TOURING CARAVANS
Electric Hook-ups
Licensed Tent Site adjoining
AMENITIES
Wash Toilet Shower Block   Shaver Points   Hair Dryers
Licensed Shop   Laundry   Café / Coffee Shop
Cycle Compound

Please phone or send for free brochure
SCOTGATE CHALET, CAMPING &
CARAVAN HOLIDAY PARK
Braithwaite, Keswick, Cumbria CA12 5TF
Tel   017687 78343
Fax 017687 78099

ARRAGONS CYCLE CENTRE
2 Brunswick Road
Penrith

Your Coast to Coast Cycle Shop
For spares, repairs, wheel-building
and wheel repairs

Main agents for
**MARIN SARACEN DAWES
RALEIGH**

Any problems at all,
just give us a call

01768   890344

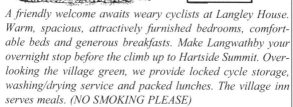

ST PAUL'S MISSION
ALSTON

Open from 1st April 1998, St Paul's Mission is a facility custom made for C2C participants in a converted Chapel.

Our range of indoor amenities include:
Bunk-bed accommodation for 36 guests (bunk-beds in separate cubicles), large showering and WC facilities, indoor bike security room, launderette, sauna, kitchen with cooking facilities, food and drinks available, lounge with pool table, TV, full central heating, cinema under construction upstairs for completion 2000. Telephone for a full colour brochure.

Rates

Bed only	£10.00
Bed (sleeping bag + pillow)	£15.00

Please book in advance: **St Paul's Mission**
Town Head   Alston   CA9 3SL
01434 382441 or Fax 01434 382441

83

BEE COTTAGE FARM

CASTLESIDE CONSETT
CO. DURHAM DH8 9HW
Tel Liz Lawson 01207 508224
Farmhouse Teas
Bed & Breakfast
Self-catering

A working farm with lovely views situated close to the Waskerley Way
(between points 105 and 106 on the C2C map.)

Evening Meals and Packed Lunches available
Tea-Room open 1 - 6pm

Good food - plenty of it!

A warm, friendly welcome and home comforts
for individual cyclists, family groups
or even larger parties
Sleeps 34

The "Wish You Were Here" TV team stayed with us whilst in the area when making the C2C film - *We hope you will too!*

English Tourist Board
HIGHLY COMMENDED

Highly Commended

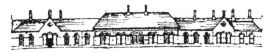

TYNEMOUTH STATION URBAN BOTHY

Residential accommodation within the station building conveniently situated adjacent to the main square, village centre, shops and pubs. The Metro stops at the station, giving access to Newcastle and coastal resorts.

This facility is ideally situated, being at the end of the Sea to Sea (C2C) route, at the beginning of the Reivers cycle route (return C2C), at the end/beginning of the Newcastle to Carlisle, and the Coast and Castles (Tynemouth to Berwick). The official accreditation stamp is obtained by calling at the Bothy or Porters, both within the station.

The facility provides bunk-beds, showers, WC, H & C, CH, bike store (breakfast and snacks available from adjacent Coffee Shop)

2000 price guide
Single bed, per night using own sleeping bag £9.00
Bed and breakfast, inclusive rate £15.00

Anew facility which opened in 1998. Party/Group enquiries are welcome as well as individual bookings. For further information please send a SAE to **Ray Demesne, The Estate Office, Kirkwhelpington, Northumberland NE19 2RG Tel 01830 540342 For reservations telephone the Bothy on 0191 258 3167**

**TYNEMOUTH STATION
STATION TERRACE
TYNEMOUTH
TYNE & WEAR
NE30 4RE**

The Reivers Cycle Route

A cycle Route
from
Tynemouth to Whitehaven

To be used with the official route map
available from Sustrans 0117 929 0888

Gina Farncombe

Curlew Press

The Reivers Cycle Route

This 150 mile cycle way runs from east to west coast with the gradients in the cyclist's favour. It winds its way through some of the wildest and most untouched countryside in the UK from the mouth of the mighty River Tyne to the Cumbrian coast. Along the way riders will follow the shores of beautiful Kielder Water before crossing the border for a brief foray into Scotland.

The Route has been named after the marauding family clans who terrorised northern England and the Scottish Borders in the 15th c. and 16th c. They lived by cattle rustling, kidnapping, arson and murder. The route passes many fortified farmhouses revealing the rich heritage of the area.

The Reivers Cycle Route gives the potential of a wonderful round trip by linking with the C2C at Whitehaven.

Start your holiday from home by leaving your car behind! There are frequent main line inter-city trains to and from Newcastle.

If at all possible, please book accommodation, meals and packed lunches in advance, and do not arrive unannounced expecting beds and meals to be available! If you have to cancel a booking, please give the proprietor as much notice as you can so that the accommodation can be re-let.

Note   Back-up vehicles are strongly advised to use main roads in order to keep the Reivers Cycle Route as traffic free as possible.

Contents

Accommodation
place names (east-west)

REIVERS CYCLE ROUTE - WESTERN HALF

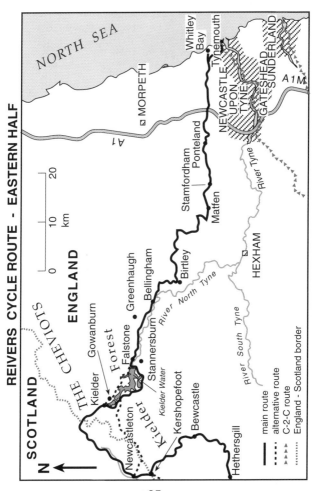

REIVERS CYCLE ROUTE - EASTERN HALF

NORTH SEA

N

SCOTLAND

THE CHEVIOTS

ENGLAND

Kielder Forest

Kielder

Gowanburn

Falstone

Greenhaugh

Bellingham

Stannersburn

Kielder Water

Newcastleton

Kershopefoot

Bewcastle

Hethersgill

Morpeth

Whitley Bay

Tynemouth

NEWCASTLE UPON TYNE

GATESHEAD

SUNDERLAND

A1M

A1

Ponteland

Stamfordham

Matfen

Birtley

River North Tyne

River Tyne

River South Tyne

HEXHAM

km
0   10   20

main route
alternative route
C-2-C route
England - Scotland border

95

NEWCASTLE

Newcastle can trace its beginnings to the river-crossing and fort which we know as the start of Hadrian's Wall. Later Robert, the son of William I, built a fort in 1080 and called it Newcastle. The shipping of coal and wool played a big part in the town's growth as a merchant and trading centre, and later ship-building and engineering were to employ a large part of the community.

TYNEMOUTH owes its existence to the outcrop of hard sandstone which juts out be-

Earl Grey Monument

tween the Tyne and the sea defying the effects of wave and weather. Monks from the Holy Island of Lindisfarne came here in 627 and built the Priory which was one of the richest in the country and at one stage in its history monks were sent here as a reprimand for being disobedient. One poor exile wrote: "Shipwrecks are frequent and the poor people eat only a malodorous seaweed called 'slank' which they gather on the

rocks, but the church is of wondrous beauty." Later during the Roman occupation Tynemouth was an important supply port for Hadrian's Wall. In Victorian times people flocked here on the new railway to enjoy the sheltered bathing and boating.

Tynemouth Priory

NEWCASTLE

PLACES OF INTEREST
Bagpipe Museum   Unusual and interesting
Laing Art Gallery   Holds very good exhibitions

PLACES TO EAT
"Crown Posada" Pub   On quayside: lively atmosphere
Café Procope   On quayside: good food and
                         popular with students

BIKE SHOPS and REPAIRS
Hardisty Bikes   5 Union Road 0191 510 8155
Dentons   Blenheim St 0191 232 3903

TYNEMOUTH

PLACES OF INTEREST
The Castle and Priory Great atmosphere
Sea Life Centre   Excellent displays

PLACES TO EAT
Land of Green Ginger   Home-made food café
Porters Café   Tynemouth Station

OUTDOOR EQUIPMENT
Outdoor World   Whitley Bay, good stock
                           of outdoor equipment

Tynemouth and Whitley Bay

St Mary's Lighthouse

Stuart Collingwood Avalon Hotel, 26 South Parade,
Whitley Bay, Tyne & Wear NE26 2RG

Telephone	**0191 251 0080** Fax 0191 251 0100
Rooms	3 single + 2 double + 1 twin + 8 family
B&B	£20.00-£30.00
Evening Meal	7pm-8pm Packed lunch £5.00
Distance from route	On route Pub 20 yds

2 Star ETB *(See advertisement page 87.)* *"Come this way - start/finish in Whitley Bay. A quality cyclist-friendly historical family-run hotel. All rooms en-suite. Bar, restaurant."*

Marissa Ruddy   York House Hotel, 30 Park Parade,
Whitley Bay, Tyne & Wear NE26 1DX

Telephone	**0191 252 8313 Fax 0191 251 3953**
e-mail	reservation@yorkhousehotel.com
Rooms	1 single + 6 double + 7 twin + 2 family
B&B	£25.00-£30.00
Evening meal	£6.50-£12.50
Packed lunch	Available
Distance Route	On route Pub 50 yds

4 Diamonds RAC & AA *"Set in a Victorian terrace. The York House offers high standards of service combined with tastefully refurbished accommodation."*

Tynemouth and Whitley Bay

Marlborough Hotel 20 - 21 East Parade, Central Promenade, Whitley Bay NE26 1AP

Telephone	**0191 251 3628** Fax 0191 252 5033
e-mail	reception@marlboroughhotel.co.uk
Rooms	15 double/single/twin *(most en-suite)*
B&B	£22.00-£30.00
Evening meal	£11.95 Packed lunch £5.00
Distance from Route	On route

4 Diamonds ETC & AA *"An attractive well-maintained hotel situated on the promenade. A good standard of accommodation in smart modern bedrooms (2 on the ground floor)."*

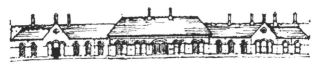

Tynemouth Station Tynemouth Station,
 Urban Bothy Station Terrace, Tynemouth NE30 4RE
Telephone **0191 258 3167**
Residential accommodation within the newly restored station building. *(See advertisement on page 89)*

Belsay

Kath Fearns Bounder House B&B, Belsay,
Northumberland NE20 OJR

Telephone **01661 881267** Mobile 0589 643664
Fax 01661 881266 e-mail: **k.fearns@bigfoot.com**
Rooms 2 doubles + 1 twin + 1 family
B&B £19.0-£20.00 Ev. meal £7.00
Packed lunch £3.00 *(prior arrangement for meal)*
Distance from route 3 miles Pub 4 miles

"Comfortable farmhouse. Quiet situation. Full central heating. Good food. Guest's lounge. B&B signed from the route - please 'phone for instructions. Lift to the pub."

Stamfordham

Mrs V. Fitzpatrick Church House, Stamfordham,
Northumberland NE18 0PB

Telephone **01661 886736** Mobile 0589 312623
Rooms 2 twin
B&B £22.00
Packed lunch £3.50-£4.50
Distance from route On route Pub nearby

"Pretty village green, old village pubs. 17th-c cream painted stone house of character on south side of green, private residence. Good breakfast, welcoming hosts."

BELLINGHAM

This ancient little market town, known locally as "Bellin-jum", nestles at the foot of some of the wildest and most barren fells in Northumberland. There are medieval references to Bellingham Castle belonging to the King of Scotland's forester, but sadly no trace remains.

Bellingham Bridge

St Cuthbert's Church is unique with its stone roof and extremely narrow windows. Both features were some defence against the marauding Scots who twice burnt it to the ground. In its graveyard lies the famous "Long Pack" which is responsible for one of Northumbrian's most notorious tales of murder, intrigue and deception.

PLACES OF INTEREST
Hareshaw Linn   Superb waterfall, ½ mile walk
St Cuthbert's Well   Reputed to be healing water -
                             especially for sore cyclists!

PLACES TO EAT
The Cheviot Hotel   Restaurant and bar meals
Fountain Tea Room   Good cheese scones!

BIKE REPAIRS
Village Country   Do hold some spare parts
  Store   01434 220027

Bellingham

David and June Minchin
Westfield Guest House, Bellingham, Hexham, Northumberland NE48 2DP

Telephone **01434 220340** Fax 01434 220694

e-mail westfield.house@virgin.net

Rooms 2 double + 2 twin + 1 family

B&B £25.00-£28.00 *(all en-suite)*

Evening meal £15.50   Packed lunch £5.00

Distance from route On route   Pub 5 mins. walk

(No smoking please.) **4 Diamonds.** "*High quality comfortable accommodation in elegant Victorian house. Good food, relaxed atmosphere. We are well-used to drying-out drowned cyclists! Storage for cycles.*"

Mr and Mrs T.V. Forster
Crofters End, The Croft, Bellingham, Hexham, Northumberland NE48 2JY

Telephone **01434 220034**

Rooms 1 single + 1 double + 1 twin/family

B&B £16.00-£18.00

Packed lunch £3.00 *(prior notice please)*

Distance from route 100 yds   Pub ½ mile

(No smoking please.) "*End terrace family home on outskirts of village. Homely ex-farming family. Pennine Way passes the gate. We like our walkers and cyclists best!* "

Joyce Gaskin
'Lyndale' Guest House + holiday cottage Bellingham, Northumberland NE48 2AW

Telephone/Fax **01434 220361**

Rooms 1 single + 2 double + 1 twin + family

B&B £22.50-£25.00

Evening meal £12.50   Packed lunch £3.00

Distance from route On route   Pub nearby

(No smoking please.) **4 Diamonds** "*Perfect place for a welcome break. Ground floor quality en-suites. Excellent dinners & choice breafasts. Very good lock up for bikes.*"

FALSTONE

This secluded little hamlet lost nearly 80% of its parish under the waters of Kielder Reservoir. Today the village is a tranquil beauty spot surrounded by trees, and a good stopping place for the cyclist with post office, shop and pub. A tributary to the Tyne bubbles its way through the centre of the village and, depending on the time of year, it is possible to see dippers, heron, cormorants, goosanders, and with luck you may witness the miraculous sight of salmon spawning.

The Village Hall

Teas. Floor-sleeping space, cooking and washing facilities
Hylton Pyner 01434 240296

Post Office

Mrs Entwisle

The Blackcock

Old world pub with good food

Falstone

Robin Kershaw The Pheasant Inn, Stannersburn,
Falstone, Kielder Water,
Northumberland NE48 1DD

Telephone/Fax **01434 240382**
e-mail **thepheasantinn@kielderwater.demon.co.uk**
Rooms 4 doubles + 4 twins + 1 family
B&B £25.00
Evening meal £6.95, 3-course meal £12.00-£15.00
Packed lunch £5.00
Distance from route 1 mile   Public bar

(No smoking in bedrooms and dining room please.) **4 Diamonds.** *"A traditional country Inn, bursting with character. Stone walls, beams and open fires provide its cosy atmosphere. Real ale, good home-cooking, all rooms en-suite."*

Mr Ernest Swailes Falstone Village Hall, Falstone, Hexham,
Northumberland NE48 1BB

Telephone **01434 240343**

Floor space available for groups of up to 25 people. Showers, toilets, washing and cooking facilities. Bring your own sleeping bag and roll mat. Minimum charge £25.00 for up to 20 people.

**Peter and Linda
  Laws** The Blackcock Inn, Falstone, Hexham,
Nr Kielder, Northumberland NE48 1AA

Telephone/Fax **01434 240200**
Rooms 2 double + 2 twin + 1 family
B&B £20.00-£28.00
Evening meal £3.75-£10.95 Packed lunch £3.25
Distance from route On route   Public bar

(No smoking in dining-room or bedrooms please) **3 Diamonds** *"Olde world country pub with good home cooked food, real ale, comfortable accommodation. Log fires. Walkers & cyclists warmly welcomed. Bike storage available."*

Falstone

John and Shirley Richardson
High Yarrow Farm, Falstone, Hexham Northumberland NE48 1BG

Telephone **01434 240264**
Rooms 1 twin + 1 single *(no smoking please)*
B&B £16.00 Packed lunch £3.00
(prior notice for packed lunch please)
Distance from route ¼ mile Pubs nearby
Listed Commended. *"150-year-old farmhouse on working farm situated at the foot of Kielder Water in the hamlet of Yarrow. Happy to offer transport to the pub if needed"*

Mrs Karen Hodgson
Ridge End Farm, Falstone, nr Kielder Water, Hexham, NE48 1DE

Telephone **01434 240395**
Rooms 1 twin + 1 family *(both en-suite)*
B&B £20.00 *(no smoking please)*
Evening meal No Packed lunch £3.00
Distance from route ½ mile
Pub nearby

4 Diamonds *"This is a magnificent 16th-c bastel house (a fortified farmhouse). It is the historic home of border reivers and has 5ft thick walls. Private lounge available for guests with roaring log fires. There is a cottage available also."*

KIELDER WATER

A wild and romantic place, Kielder Water is the heart of Border Reiver country. It is hard to imagine the cattle rustling, kidnapping and arson that flourished here in the 15th and 16th centuries. Today Kielder's stunning scenery, peace and quiet welcome all visitors. There are a wealth of facilities for the cyclist here. Northumbria Water, who created the reservoir, has been responsible for a good deal of the inspiration behind the Reivers Cycle Route.

PLACES OF INTEREST
Tower Knowe Visitor Centre
An Information Centre with extensive gift shop and audio visual exhibition. Situated on south bank very near the dam wall.

Leaplish Waterside Park
Heated swimming pool and sauna, campsite, B&B accommodation together with a licensed restaurant, sculpture trail, bird of prey centre, and much more.

KIELDER VILLAGE

Kielder Castle

Situated at the head of the reservoir Kielder was once in a wild and uncultivated country surrounded by moors and bogs. It is now a purpose-built forestry village cocooned by alpine spruce and pine trees. Before the turn of the century Kielder Castle, which stands guard over the village, would have been hidden and alone at the valley head. It was built in 1775 by the Duke of Northumberland as his hunting lodge. Shooting parties travelled from London on the sleeper and were met at the station by pony and trap. To carry home a bag of 200 brace of grouse and blackcock in a day was not unusual. The village is a small oasis for the cyclist with a shop, pub and post office.

PLACES OF INTEREST
Kielder Castle Forest   Shop, tea room, WCs
  Park Information Centre 01434 250209

PLACES TO EAT
The Anglers Arms   01434 250234

BIKE SHOPS
Kielder Bikes   Ken and Kim Bone, opposite the
Castle **Tel. 01434 250392**

REIVERS CYCLE ROUTE - Kielder Water area

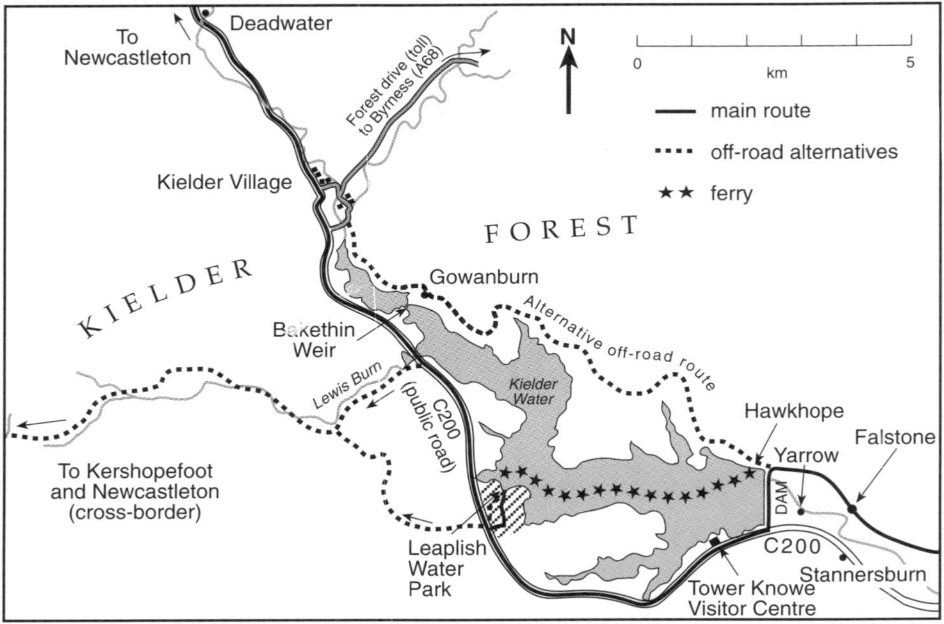

Map legend:
- main route
- off-road alternatives
- ★★ ferry

Scale: 0 — 5 km

N

FOREST

KIELDER

Locations and labels:
- To Newcastleton
- Deadwater
- Forest drive (toll) to Byrness (A68)
- Kielder Village
- Gowanburn
- Alternative off-road route
- Bakethin Weir
- Lewis Burn
- C200 (public road)
- Kielder Water
- Leaplish Water Park
- To Kershopefoot and Newcastleton (cross-border)
- Tower Knowe Visitor Centre
- C200
- Stannersburn
- DAM
- Hawkhope
- Yarrow
- Falstone

Kielder

Julia Scott Leaplish Waterside Park, Kielder
  Water, Northumberland NE48 1BT
Telephone **01434 250312** Fax 01434 250 806
e-mail kielder.water@nwl.co.uk
Rooms 2 Dormitories *(sleep 8 people in each)*
  + 2 double rooms
B&B £10.00-£20.00
Evening meal from £5.50-£15.00 Pk. lunch £4.00
Distance from route On route Pub nearby
*"The Reivers rest Bunkbarn on the Reivers Route. Dormitory, double and family rooms with en-suite. Wide range of services on site"***(see advertisement on page 125)**

Mrs Janet Scott Gowanburn, Kielder, Hexham,
  Northumberland NE48 1HL
Telephone **01434 250254**
Rooms 1 double + 1 twin + 1 family
B&B £16.50-£17.50
Evening meal Light meal Packed lunch £2.50
Distance from route On route Pub 1½ miles
Listed Commended. *"Superb views, peaceful old farmhouse on edge of Kielder Water."*

Mrs Fiona Hall Deadwater Farm, Kielder, Hexham,
  Northumberland NE48 1EW
Telephone **01434 250216**
Rooms 1 double + 1 twin + 1 family
B&B £16.00
Evening meal Snack £4.00 Packed lunch £3.00
Distance from route 100 yds Pub 2½ miles
(No smoking except in lounge please.) **Listed.** *"Old stone-built farmhouse in peaceful surroundings on Scotland/England border. It is recommended to eat on way here, unless you require a small meal.. Bunk house at Leaplish too!"*

NEWCASTLETON

Newcastleton, with its broad Georgian streets and open squares, was purpose designed and built from scratch by the Duke of Buccleugh in 1792. Due to the changes in agriculture there was a need for more village-based employment such as handloom weaving. They were built with large windows to let in light for the new cottage industries.

The town has a post office, several pubs, a wonderfully eccentric combined tea and antique shop and several guesthouses. If your time and energy allow don't miss a short detour to Hermitage Castle. This mysterious and magical place not only witnessed long years of turbulent border reiving, but

it played host to the tragic Mary Queen of Scots when she snatched two hours' rendezvous with her lover Boswell.

Hermitage Castle

Newcastleton

Helen Rabour   Woodside, North Hermitage Street, Newcastleton,Roxburghshire TD9 0RZ

Telephone/Fax   **013873 75431**

E-mail: helenrabour@woodsideborders.freeserve.co.uk

Rooms   2 double + 2 twin + 1 single

B&B   £16.00

Evening meal   from £3.00   Packed lunch £3.00

Distance from route   On route   Pub nearby

"Large house at north end of village. Spacious rooms with good beds & good food. Licensed. Also safe bike storage."

Bailey Mill

Mrs Pamela Copeland   Bailey Mill Accommodation & Trekking, Bailey, Newcastleton, Roxburghshire TD9 0TR

Telephone/Fax   **016977 48617**

e-mail   **lindastenhouse@virgin.co.uk**

Rooms   2 single + 4 double + 4 twin + 2 family

B&B   £20.00-£28.00

Evening meal   £8.00 Packed lunch £2.00

Distance from route   On route   Pub on site

3 Key Commended. *"Courtyard apartments for self-catering or B&B. Relax in our Jacuzzi, sauna, steam shower, then enjoy a drink and meal, delivered to your apartment or in our licensed bar."*

Askerton Castle

BEWCASTLE

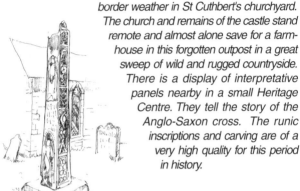

The famous Bewcastle Cross has survived 1300 years of relentless border weather in St Cuthbert's churchyard. The church and remains of the castle stand remote and almost alone save for a farm-house in this forgotten outpost in a great sweep of wild and rugged countryside. There is a display of interpretative panels nearby in a small Heritage Centre. They tell the story of the Anglo-Saxon cross. The runic inscriptions and carving are of a very high quality for this period in history.

'Summer is for grazing, but autumn is for raiding'

Just like football, our raiding friends were far too busy tending crops and fattening the cattle in summer to be doing any reiving, but as soon as the crops were gathered and the horses fit they would be hot foot across whichever border to get down to the serious winter business of stealing each other's wives, girl-friends, cattle, sheep and care-fully-stored winter goods again.

Walton

Mrs Una Armstrong

	Town Head Farm, Walton, nr Brampton, Cumbria CA8 2DJ
Telephone	**016977 2730**
Rooms	1 double + 1 family
B&B	£15.00
Evening meal	6pm-6.30pm Packed lunch £3.00
Distance from route	400 yds Pub 400 yds

(No smoking in bedrooms please.) **3 Diamonds** *"Cosy farmhouse with friendly atmosphere on working mixed farm. Overlooks village green with play area. Picturesque views of Pennines and Lakeland hills. Hadrian's Wall nearby."*

Mrs Margaret Mounsey

	Walton High Rigg, Walton, Brampton, Cumbria CA8 2AZ
Telephone	**016977 2117**
Rooms	1 family/double
B&B	£16.00
Evening meal	£9.00 *(pre-book please)*
Packed lunch	£3.00
Distance from route	3/4 mile Pub 3/4 mile

(No smoking please.) **3 Diamonds.** *"Comfortable spacious 18th-c farmhouse, friendly family dairy/ sheep farm one mile from Roman Wall, 3/4 mile Walton village. Good local knowledge. Bikes safely stored. Delicious home cooking. Lifts to pub."*

Catlowdy near Longtown

Jack and **Margaret Sisson**	Bessietown Farm Country Guesthouse, Catlowdy, Longtown, Carlisle CA6 5QP
Telephone/Fax	**01228 577219 + 577019**
Rooms	2 single + 4 double + 4 twin + 2 family
B&B	£22.50-£23.50 *(no smoking please)*
Evening meal	£11.00
Distance from route	1½ miles Pub 6 miles

3 Crowns Highly Commended, AA QQQQQ. *"Warm welcome and delicious food. Drinks licence. All rooms en-suite Indoor heated swimming pool open May to mid-September."*

Jane Lawson	Craigburn Farm, Catlowdy, nr Longtown, Carlisle CA6 5QP
Telephone	**01228 577214 Fax 577014**
e-mail	louiselawson@hotmail.com
Rooms	2 double + 3 twin + 1 family *(all en-suite)*
B&B	£22.00 *(no smoking in bedrooms please)*
Evening meal	£12.00 Packed lunch £3.50
Distance from route	2 miles Pub 3 miles

3 Diamonds *"Friendly relaxed atmosphere. Some four-poster beds. Tea/coffee and TV. Delicious home-cooking, desserts a speciality. Licensed. Credit cards accepted."*

Catlowdy near Longtown

Ruth Casson Liddel Lodge, Catlowdy, Penton, nr Carlisle, Cumbria CA6 5QN

Telephone **01228 577335**
Rooms 1 single + 1 double + 1 family
B&B £17.00-£18.00 *(no smoking please)*
Evening meal £10.00 Packed lunch £5.00
Distance from route ¼ miles Pub 2½ miles

ETB 2 Crowns commended. *"Hunting lodge with panoramic views of Liddesdale. Excellent base for exploring the Borders. Home-produce and cooking. Brochure available."*

Kirklinton

Margaret Harrison Clift House Farm, Kirklinton, (Near Smithfield) Carlisle, Cumbria, CA6 6DE.

Telephone **01228 675237**
Mobile 07771 520 984
Rooms 1 double + 2 twin
B&B £17.00-£19.00 Evening meal
Pub Nearby
Distance from route On route

ETB 3 Diamonds *"Spacious friendly farmhouse on the banks of the river Lyne. Beautiful walks and fishing. Complimentary tea and home baking on arrival. Brochure available."*

CARLISLE

This great border city greets its guests with open arms, but not so many years ago any visitor would have been treated with suspicion. It was the nerve-centre for bitter feuds and bloody battles created by the long-running dispute over the border betwen England and Scotland. Early in its history it was an important Roman headquarters for Hadrian's Wall. In 1092 William the Conqueror's son started to build the castle where later the unfortunate Mary Queen of Scots was incarcerated.

PLACES OF INTEREST

Tullie House Museum and Art Gallery	Excellent audio-visual interpretation of the Border Reivers
Carlisle Castle	Medieval dungeons, exhibitions
Carlisle Cathedral	Founded in 1122, fine wood carving and wall panels

PLACES TO EAT

The GrapeVine	Excellent, value for money, vegetarian food 01228 546617
Ottakers	**Town centre. Exciting & novel book shop with excellent cafe.**

BIKE REPAIRS

Palace Cycle	122 Botchergate 01228 523142
Scotby Cycles	Bridge St 01228 546931

Carlisle

Geoff and Elaine Webster Angus Hotel, 14 Scotland Road, Carlisle CA3 9DG
Telephone **01228 523546**
e-mail **angusandalmonds@enterprise.net**
Rooms 3 single + 4 double + 3 family + 4 twin
B&B £20.00-£27.00
Evening meal £10.00-£18.00 Pck. lunch£3.50-£5.00
Distance from route On route

(Mainly a non-smoking hotel.) **4 Diamonds.** *"Cosy Victorian town house offering personal hospitality, superb food in Almonds Bistro, local cheeses, home-baked bread and draught beer. Secure car parking and cycle storage."*
(See advertisement on page 125)

Eric and Daphne Houghton Cherry Grove, 87 Petteril Street, Carlisle, Cumbria CA1 2AW
Telephone/Fax **01228 541942**
e-mail **petteril87@aol.com**
Rooms 2 double + 3 twin
B&B £20.00-£25.00
Packed lunch £3.75
Distance from route On route   Pub nearby

3 Diamonds *"Comfortable family run guest house with newly refurbished rooms .All rooms en-suite with all facilities including hairdryer and Satellite TV. Good English breakfast, easy walking distance of city centre."*

Carlisle

Tina Murray Parkland Guest House, 136 Petteril
Street,Carlisle, Cumbria CA1 2AW
Telephone/Fax **01228 548331**
Rooms 2 double + 3 twin + 1 family room
B&B £17.50-£20.00
Packed lunch £6.00
Distance from route On route Pub nearby

3 Diamonds *"Comfortable family run guest house with newly refurbished rooms .All rooms en-suite with all facilities including hairdryer and Satellite TV. Good English breakfast, easy walking distance of city centre. Very near bus and train stations."*

Sheila Nixon No. 1 Etterby Street Carlisle,
Cumbria CA3 9JB
Telephone/Fax **01228 547285**
Mobile **078 999 48711**
Rooms 1 double + 2 single rooms
B&B £18.00
Evening meal £5.00-£8.00 *(prior notice please)*
Packed lunch £3.00
Distance from route On route Pub nearby

3 Diamonds *"We are situated near the city centre. There is secure cycle storage and we offer good wholesome food and a warm welcome will await you."*

THE EASTERN FELLS OF THE LAKE DISTRICT NATIONAL PARK

Tread softly as you pass through this miraculously untouched corner of England!

St Mungo hurried here in the 6th century, for he had heard muffled whispers that word of the Gospels had not reached the ears of the wild and unruly people living in the Eastern Fells! Many of the local churches are named after his other more formal name, St Kentigern.

HESKET NEWMARKET

Ask a local inhabitant the name of an ash tree and he will tell you it is a 'Hesh'. Hesket means the place of the ash trees. Local farmers bought and sold bulls at the market cross. A generous village green invites travellers to taste the local brewed beer and rest awhile. There is a well stocked village shop, a post office, pub and several guest-houses. The Crown Inn is famous for its own home-brewed ales. They are named after local fells: Blencathra, Great Cock-up, and Doris in honour of the landlord's mother on her 90th birthday.

Hesket-New-Market

Margaret Monkhouse

	Denton House, Hesket-New-Market, nr Caldbeck, Cumbria CA7 8JG
Telephone	**016974 78415**
Rooms	1 single + 2 double + 2 twin + 2 family
B&B	£20.00-£23.00
Evening meal	£8.50-£10.00
Packed lunch	£3.00 *(prior notice please)*
Distance from route	On route
Pub	Nearby *(with own brewery)*

(No smoking in bedrooms please.) "Warm family atmosphere welcomes everyone, with log fires and home-cooking. Most rooms are en-suite."

Mrs Dorothy Studholme

	Newlands Grange, Hesket-New-Market, nr Wigton, Cumbria CA7 8HP
Telephone	**016974 78676**
Rooms	1 single + 2 double + 2 twin/family
B&B	£16.50-£19.00
Evening meal	£7.50 Packed lunch £3.00
Distance from route	On route Pub 1½ miles

"Newlands Grange is a working farm looking onto the Caldbeck Fells, house featuring old oak beams and open fire. Good home-cooking and a warm welcome awaits all."

CALDBECK

Named after the river (Cold-beck), Caldbeck was a thriving rural industrial centre before steam-power and the Industrial Revolution. There is still a clog-maker in the village centre. In 1800 there were no fewer than 8 water-powered mills   making bobbins, woollens and grinding corn.

***The Priests Mill** which has been beautifully restored houses a craft centre, display area and restaurant with a   picture gallery.*
In the churchyard is John Peel's grave , the famous Cumbrian Huntsman, and that of Mary, the Beauty of Buttermere who was the subject of the novel 'The Maid of Buttermere' by Melvyn Bragg.

PLACES OF INTEREST
The Howk   A hidden gem upstream from the village
The Clog Maker   Will Strong: next to the bridge

PLACES TO EAT
Priests Mill   Delicious vegetarian food: you'll return!
Odd Fellows Arms Wholesome country food

*After Caldbeck the route winds its way round the fell: an area known locally as Back 'a Skiddaw. **Parkend Restaurant** and **The Snooty Fox** are the only watering holes for several miles.*

Caldbeck

Mrs Nan Savage	Swaledale Watch, Whelpo, nr Caldbeck, Wigton, Cumbria CA7 8HQ
Telephone/Fax	**016974 78409**
Rooms	2 double + 1 twin + 2 family
B&B	£17.00-£21.00
Evening meal	£11.00 *(served on Tues, Wed, Thu and Sat, prior notice please)*
Packed lunch	£3.50 approx *(prior notice please)*
Distance from route	On route Pub 1 mile

AA Selected QQQQ. *"Enjoy great comfort in beautiful surroundings on our working farm. A warm welcome, hot bath and good food awaits you. First there gets the Jacuzzi!"*

Mrs C. Slinger	Parkend Restaurant & Country Hotel, nr Caldbeck, Wigton, Cumbria CA7 8HH
Telephone	**016974 78494** Fax 016974 78580
Rooms	4 double + 2 twin
B&B	£25.00-£32.00
Evening meal	£4.50-£20.00 Packed lunch £4.50
Distance from route	¼ mile Licensed bar

(No smoking in dining room please.) **2 Star Hotel** *"17th-c farmhouse restaurant with quality en-suite rooms. Fine food in tranquil surroundings. Lock up bike park."*

For tourist information and accommodation in Cockermouth please turn to pages 18 - 20

Useful Telephone Numbers

Weather News

North East England Weathercall   0891 500 418
Cumbria & the Lake District Weathercall   0891 500 419

Tourist Information Centres

Gateshead   0191 477 3478
Newcastle-upon-Tyne   0191 261 0610
Whitley Bay   0191 200 8535
Hawick   01450 372547
Bellingham   01434 220616
Kielder   01434 240398
Longtown   01228 792835
Carlisle   01228 625600
Cockermouth   01900 822634
Silloth-on-Solway   01697 331944
Whitehaven   01946 695678
Maryport   01900 813738

Travel Information: Bus, Coach and Train

Northumberland County Council   01670 533128
Tyne & Wear County Council Travellink   0191 232 5325
Stagecoach Cumberland   01946 63222
National Express   0990 808080
National Express Newcastle   0191 232 3300
National Rail Enquiries Line   0345 484 950
Scotrail Enquiries Line   0345 550033
Cycle Booking Line NW Trains   0161 228 5906

How to get Home

Holiday Lakeland *(see inside cover)*   016973 71871
Stanley Taxis *(see page 90)*   01207 237424

Ted Gilman *(see page 126)*   0191 286 7534

Bike Shops and Repairs

Tynemouth   Cyclepath, 14 Queensway 0191 258 6600

Metro Centre The Bike Place, 8 Allison Court 0191 488 3137

Newcastle   Newcastle Cycle Centre, 165 Westgate Rd
0191 230 3022
Dentons, Blenheim St 0191 232 3903

Byker   Hardisty Cycles, 5 Union Rd 0191 265 8619

Bellingham   Village and Country Store do some spare
parts 01434 220027

Kielder   Kielder Castle, Ken and Kim Bone
01434 250392

Carlisle   Mike Lee, Palace Cycle Stores, 122 Botchergate
01228 523142
Scotby Cycles, Bridge Street
01228 546931

Cockermouth   Derwent Cycles 01900 822113
The Wordsworth Hotel
Bike Hire 01900 822757